Media and Society

The R&L Series in Mass Communication
Eileen Meehan, Louisiana State University, Series Editor

Rowman & Littlefield is pleased to announce a series of texts for mass communication courses. Edited by Eileen Meehan, Louisiana State University, and advised by an editorial board representing a cross section of universities and specialties, the series consists of "compact core" textbooks, around 200–250 pages each, providing clear and concise overviews of key areas of mass communication study. These accessible and engaging texts feature illustrations, pedagogical tools, and practical guidelines to show students how to apply concepts outside the classroom.

Future topics in the series may include media and politics, law, ethics, international communication, online communication, mass communication theory, research methods, economics, gender and media, comparative media systems, new communications technology, history, media effects, policy and regulation, management, advertising, public relations, popular culture, film, visual communication, and media literacy.

Editorial Board

Titles in the Series

Media and Society: A Critical Perspective
Arthur Asa Berger

MEDIA AND SOCIETY

A Critical Perspective

ARTHUR ASA BERGER

ROWMAN & LITTLEFIELD PUBLISHERS, INC.
Lanham • Boulder • New York • Toronto • Oxford

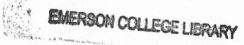

ROWMAN & LITTLEFIELD PUBLISHERS, INC.

Published in the United States of America
by Rowman & Littlefield Publishers, Inc.
A wholly owned subsidiary of The Rowman & Littlefield
Publishing Group, Inc.
4501 Forbes Boulevard, Suite 200, Lanham, Maryland 20706
www.rowmanlittlefield.com

P.O. Box 317, Oxford OX2 9RU, United Kingdom

British Library Cataloguing in Publication Information Available

Library of Congress Cataloging-in-Publication Data

Berger, Arthur Asa, 1933–
  Media and society : a critical perspective / Arthur Asa Berger.
    p.   cm.—(R & L series in mass communication)
  Includes bibliographical references and index.
  ISBN 0-7425-2511-2 (cloth)—ISBN 0-7425-2512-0 (pbk.)
    1. Mass media—Social aspects. I. Title. II. Series.
HM1206.B47 2003
302.23—dc21   2003008612

Printed in the United States of America

∞ ™ The paper used in this publication meets the minimum requirements of American National Standard for Information Sciences—Permanence of Paper for Printed Library Materials, ANSI/NISO Z39.48-1992.

CONTENTS

ACKNOWLEDGMENTS

I would like to thank my editor at Rowman & Littlefield, Brenda Hadenfeldt, and the series editor, Eileen Meehan, for their help. I appreciate their continued support and the many useful suggestions they made over the course of writing this book. I also want to thank two reviewers of my manuscript, whose names I do not know, but whose comments were quite helpful. My appreciation also goes to production editor Alden Perkins, copyeditor Christianne Thillen, and everyone else involved with making this book.

I've made use of some material I previously wrote, generally in modified and adapted versions, that appeared in my various books and articles. I also made extensive use of material on the Internet that I was able to find using Google and other search engines.

Introduction

THE MEDIA AND YOU—
A CONSIDERATION

One night in 2003 a young college student—let's call him Johnny Q. Public—turned on his television set to watch an episode of *Friends*. This action, which is similar to what millions of us do every day when we "watch television" involves the following:

- a **medium**—television, that "carries" the program
- a **text**—the situation comedy *Friends*. I will adapt the convention used in academic discourse and call television programs, films, print advertisements, commercials and the like "texts."
- a product of the work of many different kinds of **artists** such as actors, actresses, producers, directors, camera-persons, and script writers
- a member of an **audience**—Johnny Q. Public (or his girlfriend Tiffany Greatgal)
- an audience that is part of a larger entity, namely a **society.**

Let's assume that Johnny Q. Public is a citizen of the United States of America—that is, he's an American. (I will generally use the term *American* in this book to stand for the United States so I don't have to keep writing *the United States* all the time. And when I write *society* I will be discussing American society, unless otherwise noted.) Audiences are parts of a larger entity, namely society—not everyone in a

1

given society watches the same program on television at any given time during the day or night (and not everyone watching a television program in America is a citizen).

FOCAL POINTS IN THE
STUDY OF MASS MEDIA

What we have here are what I call the **focal points** that can be used in dealing with the media in a given society. For the sake of alliteration, to help you remember most of these focal points, I will use words that begin with an "A" for four of them. We have, then, Art works (texts), Audiences, Artists, (the United States of) America, and some Medium. All of these are, or can be, connected to each other. For example, there are interrelationships that exist between a text carried on television, the artists who are involved in creating and performing it, the medium in which the text is carried, the audience for whom the text is created, and the society in which the audience lives. Depending on our interests, we can focus on one or more of these focal points in studying the media.

Since this book deals with the social aspects of the mass media, it will focus on the medium, audiences, and society—but it will also have a good deal to say about mass mediated texts and media artists. We must always keep in mind that the media carry texts and not neglect these texts due to our fascination with social, political, economic, and cultural matters related to the media. We also must remember that the media affect the texts they carry. In some cases audiences are global, which means "society" expands from, say, the United States, to other countries and in some cases—such as in the broadcast of the Super Bowl football game—much of the world.

FRIENDS AND THE FOCAL POINTS

Let's take an episode of the situation comedy *Friends* and plug it into the focal points chart. This may help you see more clearly what I'm talking about.

art work	*Friends* (an episode of)
audience	General public
medium	Television
artist	Writers, Production Staff, Directors, and Performers
America	(and other countries in many cases)

Writers (and artists of all kinds) always must think of their audiences. For example, my most immediate audience for this book is college students taking media courses in the United States, but I hope the book might be adopted in other countries as well. When I wrote this book I had a specific audience in mind—people like you, my reader—who I assume are undergraduates taking courses on media or communication in colleges and universities. If I had a different audience I was trying to reach—for example, Ph.D. candidates in communication—I would have written it in a much different manner. So the potential audience affects the way books are written and, by extension, the way all texts carried by the mass media are created.

I think you can see from this example that there are many different topics to consider when dealing with media and society. There is a logical problem involved with writing about the media and society—where do you best deal with a particular topic, since some topics could be put in any number of different places? For example, where do you write about media ethics—in a chapter on media, on society, or on media artists and creators?

In this book, I put my discussion of media ethics in the chapter on artists and creators, since they are the people who most directly face ethical problems in creating their texts. Is it ethical to make a print advertisement for cigarettes? Is it ethical to make a television commercial that slanders and lies about a political figure? Is it ethical to write a television script or make a movie or video game full of gratuitous violence? These are problems that artists and creators face, even though there may be other people and other factors involved—such as the people who work for the networks that carry violent shows. I have tried to place the topics where I thought they best fit.

After reading this book I hope you will have a better understanding of the role that the media and the texts they carry have played (and continue to play) in your life, in the lives of your friends and the members of your family, and in the society in which you find yourself. Although you may make individual choices of what media to consume (and what other things to consume), your decisions are affected by demographic factors such as your age, socioeconomic class, gender, educational level, and zip code, among other things. You may not realize it, but you fit into certain marketing categories; thus your behavior is, in a certain sense, predictable. For example, if you are 18–34, live in an upscale area, are college educated and white, you are a typical member of the *Friends* audience, according to the Nielsen ratings.

TWO ANECDOTES ON CHOICE

This matter of our behavior being predictable is quite interesting, and extends to realms other than choosing films to see or television programs to watch. In the summer of 2002 my wife and I took a cruise from San Francisco to Alaska and back. During the cruise we were given a tour of the ship's galley. The maître d' who was leading the tour told us that the cruise line was able to predict, with remarkable accuracy, what people would choose to eat at every meal. Long experience had taught them what to expect.

Thus, at a given dinner, while there may have been five main courses, the ships' cooks knew that 80 percent of the diners would order a certain main course, 10 percent would order a different main course, and so on. This anecdote serves as a metaphor for our understanding media usage. We can choose anything we like (given what is available, that is) but we tend to like certain programs, depending upon our demographic and psychographic profiles.

Age is an important factor. In 1984 I was a visiting professor at the Annenberg School for Communication at the University of Southern California. I had a large class of 200 students taking a course in popular culture. I brought a number of visitors from the media world to speak to my students. One visitor was a vice president of an easy-listening station. When I introduced him and mentioned the station where he worked, my students all laughed.

"That's all right," he said. "You're laughing now, but when you're forty years old you'll be listening to my station. And I've got statistics to prove it." So the music we like when we are twenty may not be the music we like when we are forty, and the same applies to all the media.

Scenes with alcohol, tobacco, and/or illicit drugs are present in seven out of ten prime-time network dramatic programs. Scenes of drinking alcoholic beverages are seen an average of every twenty minutes. . . . More major characters in prime-time television drink alcoholic beverages than anything else. . . . Female smokers now outnumber male smokers among major characters in prime-time television. . . . In a sample of the 40 highest-grossing movie titles for the years 1994 through 1995, 39 (97.5 percent) contain portrayals of alcohol, smoking, and/or illicit drugs. Those who view the most popular music video channel see alcohol use an average of every fourteen minutes, tobacco use every twenty-five minutes, and illicit drugs every forty minutes. . . . The use of addictive substances is shown as generally risk-free. More than nine out of ten drinkers, more than eight out of ten smokers, and six out of ten illicit drug users experience positive health effects or no health effects. . . . Addictive substances appear much more frequently in movies and music videos than on prime-time television. Only one of the forty movies surveyed does not have scenes involving alcohol, tobacco, and/or illegal drugs. . . . Two titles do not include any portrayal of alcohol, and six titles do not have any smoking. Illicit drug scenes are present in over one-third of the movies, more than twice their presence on prime-time television. . . . A child who grows up watching only three hours of prime-time television a day on one channel will have watched 32,000 characters who demonstrate tobacco as a part of their lives. Over 2,500 tobacco smokers will have been playing central roles in the stories being told. Yet the story of the negative health effects and addiction is not one of them. The child will have to view 2,200 smokers on television before seeing one who experiences negative health effects. (2001: 69–70, 73,75)

—George Gerbner, "Drugs in Television, Movies, and Music Videos," in Y. R. Kamalipour & K. R. Rampal, *Media, Sex, Violence, and Drugs in the Global Village*

1

MEDIA IN OUR
THOUGHTS AND LIVES

A Psychosocial Perspective on Individuals,
Society, and the Media

Although I've never met you, my reader, there are certain things I *think* I know about you. There is one important qualification I must make, however—I must assume that you are a typical American college student taking a course that deals, one way or another, with media and society. Before I tell you what I might know about you, let me begin by telling a story involving Johnny Q. Public, who I imagine is someone probably very much like you.

JOHNNY Q. PUBLIC'S MEDIA USAGE

The hero of this story is Johnny Q. Public, who lives in Normal City, USA. His apartment is about thirty minutes' drive from Central State University, where he is a junior majoring in media studies. At 7:30 a.m. Johnny's clock radio turns on. It is broadcasting a news show that has information on traffic and a weather report every ten minutes. Johnny opens the door of his apartment and gets the morning newspaper. He takes a shower, brushes his teeth, and glances at the newspaper while he has breakfast. Then he jumps in his car to drive to Central State University, in time (or maybe a few minutes late) for his 9:00 a.m. class. He listens to the radio while he is driving. He's done with classes by 2:00 p.m. and goes to his part-time job at a gym, where he is a trainer. He works until 5:00 p.m. At the gym, popular music is played over the loudspeaker system. Johnny drives back to his apartment, listening to the radio again, and gets home by 5:30 p.m. He turns on his television set and cooks dinner. He watches television while he eats. He does an hour of homework while listening to some CDs on his stereo. Then he calls his girlfriend, Tiffany Great-gal, and they agree to go to the movies Friday night. He then turns on his television set and watches for three or four hours. After watching David Letterman, he checks his e-mail on the Internet. Next he plays a video game for half an hour. Finally, he washes up, makes sure his clock radio alarm is set for the right time, and goes to bed late at night. He has spent close to the average of nine hours per day that Americans spend with media of one kind or another. When he wakes up the next morning, he wonders, "Why am I so tired?"

During the course of a normal day, Johhny has listened to the radio for a couple of hours, watched television for three or four hours, listened to music at work and on his stereo for an hour or so, spent some time on the Internet, played a video game, and spent fifteen or twenty minutes reading a newspaper. Johnny's media usage is probably a bit less than most people's because he attends college and has a part-time job, but he's pretty close to the average.

A GROUP PORTRAIT OF MY READERS

Given the fact that you are reading this book, I can make the following assumptions about you. There is a good possibility that:

- You are between 17 and 25 years old.
- You are studying at a college or university.
- You grew up watching three or four hours of television a day, on average.
- You have been subjected to hundreds of thousands of print advertisement and television and radio commercials over the last ten or fifteen years.

- You believe that while you are aware of these commercials, they do not influence your decision making in important ways.
- You believe that while you "consume" eight or nine hours of media each day, your media diet doesn't have a significant impact on your life.
- You also listen to the radio two or three hours each day and probably have some kind of gizmo that plays the kind of music you like when you're not at home.
- You use a computer to do things such as write letters, notes, term papers, and other reports; keep journals; and send e-mail to friends.
- You believe in "individualism," whatever that means, though you may not know where the term comes from.

Of course, I could be all wrong. You could be a precocious fourteen-year-old or a seventy-five-year-old retired person, and you don't watch television or listen to the radio, and you hate popular music. Instead, you spend your days reading poetry and listening to chamber music. You might have checked this book out of the library; or an older brother or sister has it, and you noticed it and picked it up because you're interested in media—because you suspect that some media may, in some way, be having some kind of an effect on your life.

It could be that you don't even know who Britney Spears is. But I doubt it.

These assumptions I made are based on data that researchers have accumulated about media usage in the United States. (The Kaiser Family Foundation issued a report containing statistics for media use from November 1998 through April 1999. The data can be found at www.-kff.org/content/1999/1535/.) A fact sheet that summarizes the findings of this research shows:

Average amount of time children spend with media each day:

5:29 hours	All kids
3:34 hours	2–7 year olds
6:43 hours	8 and older

Average amount of time children spend each day:

2:46 hours	watching television (19:19 hours a week)
1:27 hours	listening to music (10:04 hours a week)
:44 hours	reading for fun (5:15 hours a week)
:39 hours	watching videos (around 5:00 hours a week)
:21 hours	using a computer for fun (2:29 hours a week)
:20 hours	playing video games (2:20 hours a week)

Researchers found that the average young person in the United States spends from six to nine hours a day with various kinds of media, such as television, radio, recorded music, newspapers, magazines, books, and video games. That adds up to around 2,500 hours of media usage a year. Contrast that with a typical course in a university that is around 45 hours for a semester and you see how important a place media, of all kinds, has in most young people's lives. Children eight to eighteen have the following in their bedrooms: 65 percent a television set, 75 percent a CD player, and 45 percent a video-game player. The bedrooms of our children have become media emporia, so to speak.

Data from Student Monitor, a market research firm, indicates there are more than 15 million students in two- and four-year colleges and graduate schools in the United States, and these students

Figure 1.1   U.S. children spend about 2.5 hours per week using a computer.

Websites on Children and Media

Here are some other websites devoted to children and media:
  www.caru.org/
  http://pbskids.org/dontbuyit/
  http://interact.uoregon.edu/MediaLit/mlr/home/index.html
  www.childrennow.org/links/links-media.html

---

have a purchasing power of some $270 billion. According to a report by Teenage Research Unlimited, mentioned in the January 13, 2003, issue of *The New York Times,* the average sixteen-year-old now spends $104 a week. So teenagers and college students have a lot of money, and the advertising agencies and marketers are out to do what they can to channel this money into spending for the "right" things—that is, the goods and services that these agencies are selling, such as clothes, fast foods, diet foods, CDs, and going to the movies.

Figure 1.2   Teenagers are a major market segment for the movie industry and advertisers.

MEDIA EFFECTS AND YOUR LIFE

If I were to ask you, "What effect has the media had on your life?" you might offer the answer I mentioned earlier: "I am *aware* of the media, but I'm not *affected* by it!" I ask this question because several years ago I was interviewed by a reporter from a newspaper in New York. There had been a survey of teenagers who reported that they were "aware" of advertising but not "influenced" by it to any significant decree. The reporter thought that these teenagers were deluding themselves and wanted to know what I thought about the matter.

So the question arises—what influence (or in the language of social science, what effects) has your incredible exposure to the media had on your life—and the lives of all kinds of other people like you who, collectively, form American society, or who are members of any other society? That is the question this book will try to answer, and it will do so by looking at the role media plays in American society and the impact of American society upon the media. It is a complicated matter, but I will try to get to its heart in the pages that follow. Let me suggest one way that the media, and television, in particular, might affect some people.

TELEVISION VIEWING AND "VICIOUS" CYCLES

In his book *A Psychiatric Study of Myths and Fairy Tales,* psychiatrist Julius E. Heuscher suggests that young children who are exposed to material on television programs that is too adult for them—given their age levels and their developmental levels—become very disturbed. I am talking about stories with nasty arguments between men and women; stories full of violence; stories about broken families, divorces and infidelity, and that kind of thing.

This isn't a problem with books, because the children are not able to read material in books that will disturb them. But children can see the stories on television and follow what happened. As a result of their exposure to this material, they become upset and anxious; and this anxiety affects them as they grow older. They fear growing up and becoming adults. When they are older they become distrustful of others, especially members of the opposite sex, and avoid intimate relationships with them and with others because they are afraid that they will be rejected or that they will become involved in bad relationships—just like the people in television shows they watched when they were youngsters. This leads to a fear of marriage, to non-relational sexual behavior, and a fear of intimate relationships of all kinds.

As a result of this kind of behavior, these adults are unhappy—which leads to various kinds of escapism, which often takes the form of compulsive shopping, but especially viewing television programs, which they watch to obtain "relief." Thus they became locked in a vicious cycle. Because they have difficulty in forming relationships with others, they are lonely. To assuage this loneliness they end up watching a great deal of television, and thus they develop a kind of dependence on television—the same medium that led to their sorry state of affairs. Ironically, they become dependent for relief on the medium that actually helped cause their unhappiness and anxiety. Television provides relief; but at the same time, it reinforces their childhood fears—fears that cause their self-destructive behavior.

This kind of thing can also happen from watching movies; but as a rule children don't watch movies as much as they watch television, and movie watching is often controlled by parents while television watching often isn't. Is it possible, I ask, that you or someone you know got caught up in a vicious cycle like this? It's an interesting question to consider.

THE MEDIA IN SOCIETY

The media (*media* is the plural form of the term *medium*) are, we must remember, part of society. The media are one of many different institutions that exist within a society—*institutions* being the term sociologists use to stand for enduring entities and organizations that play an important role in maintaining society. Some of the more important institutions in modern societies are those involving education, the family, religion, politics, and of particular importance to us, the **mass** media. The media entertain us, socialize us, inform us, educate us, sell things to us (and sell us, as audiences, to advertisers), and indoctrinate us—among other things. The media help shape our identities, our attitudes toward racial and ethnic minorities, and our attitudes about sexuality. And the media have many other effects as well.

The mass communications media seem to have taken an increasingly dominant role in society in recent years; now the media seem to affect all the other institutions. Our political or governmental institutions have the legal power to help determine how the broadcasting media operate, since the airwaves are public property; but all too often it seems now that the broadcast media, thanks to the power of political advertising, are the tail that is determining where the governmental horse will go.

A CASE STUDY:
WHERE DID I GET THAT IDEA?

In the United States, where we believe in the American Dream of the "self-made" man and woman, where we believe in "individualism," many of us have a sense that we alone determine our own destiny—that we have, so to speak, the whole world in our hands. The term *individualism* was first used by Alexis de Tocqueville, a Frenchman who traveled in the United States in 1831 and wrote a fascinating book, *Democracy in America,* about American character and culture based on what he observed. He suggested that Americans were egalitarians and this egalitarianism shaped all our other values and our institutions. Thus, de Tocqueville derives our individualism from our egalitarianism:

> How it is that, in ages of equality, every man seeks for his opinions within himself: I am now to show how it is that, in the same ages, all his feelings are turned towards himself alone. *Individualism* is a novel expression, to which a novel idea has given birth. Our fathers were only acquainted with *égoisme* (selfishness). Selfishness is a passionate and exaggerated love of self, which leads a man to connect everything with himself and to prefer himself to everything in the world. Individualism is a mature and calm feeling, which disposes each member of the community to sever himself from the mass of his fellows, and to draw apart with his family and his friends; so that after he thus formed a little circle of his own, he willingly leaves society at large to itself. Selfishness originates in blind instinct: individualism proceeds from erroneous judgment more than from depraved feelings; it originates as much in deficiencies of mind as in perversity of heart.

Of course de Tocqueville, who didn't think much of our individualism, wrote before we developed our mass media. We still are individualists in America, though not in quite the same way that we were in the 1830s, when de Tocqueville visited the country. We are now immersed in media, and not all of us (especially when we grow older, get married, and have children) want to leave society to itself.

So the notion of individualism is something that we learn from American society. We are not born knowing about individualism, or the self-made man and woman, or anything else. We have to be taught about it. Some political figures who believe in a radical or extreme form of individualism argue that there's no such thing as society; it is just an abstraction, a term for a collection of individuals. (That point was made by Margaret Thatcher, when she was prime minister in England.)

Thus, ironically, people who learn about individualism from society sometimes find themselves arguing that society doesn't exist. This, in essence, is the point that the sociologist Karl Mannheim made in his book *Ideology and Utopia* when he said "strictly speaking, it is incorrect to say that the single individual thinks."

A French sociologist, Emile Durkheim, offers a solution to this matter of the complicated relationship that exists between individuals and society. He writes, in his classic work *The Elementary Forms of the Religious Life* (first translated into English and published in 1915):

> Society is a reality *sui generis;* it has its own peculiar characteristics, which are not found elsewhere and which are not met with again in the same form in all the rest of the universe. The representations which express it have a wholly different contents from purely individual ones and we may rest assured in advance that the first add something to the second.
>
> . . . Collective representations are the result of an immense cooperation, which stretches out not only into space but into time as well; to make them, a multitude of minds have associated, united and combined their ideas and sentiments; for them, long generations have accumulated their experience and their knowledge. A special intellectual activity is therefore concentrated in them which is infinitely richer and complexer than that of the individual. From that one can understand how the reason has been able to go beyond the limits of empirical knowledge. It does not owe this to any vague, mysterious virtue but simply to the fact that according to the well-known formula, man is double.

These are important points. The intellectual activity of society is much richer and more complex than an individual's intellectual activity. And this is because, Durkheim explains, we have history that enriches our thought. He continues with his analysis of the relation between the individual and society in the following manner:

> There are two beings in him: an individual being which has its foundation in the organism and the circle of whose activities is therefore strictly limited, and a social being which represents the highest reality in the intellectual and moral order that we can know by observation—I mean society. This duality of our nature has as its conse-

quence in the practical order, the irreducibility of a moral ideal to a utilitarian motive, and in the order of thought, the irreducibility of reason to individual experience. In so far as he belongs to society, the individual transcends himself, both when he thinks and when he acts.

We are all, in a certain sense, then, "double." *On the one hand, we are in society; and on the other hand, society is in us.* We have a physical body and a personality that is our own—that is, we are individuals—but we also are social animals, and much of what we think is based on this fact. We are taught in schools, we are socialized by our parents and peers and priests and pop stars (that is the media), so there is a strong social dimension to our lives, even if we believe that somehow we are self-made.

Marx explained that our consciousness is social. As he put it, in his *Selected Writings in Sociology and Social Philosophy*

> Morality, religion, metaphysics and other ideologies, and their corresponding forms of consciousness, no longer retain therefore their appearance of an autonomous existence. They have no history, no development; it is men, who in developing their material production and their material intercourse, change, along with this their real existence, their thinking and the products of their thinking. Life is not determined by consciousness, but consciousness by life. (1964: 75)

What Marx is arguing here is that life—that is, our social existence—shapes our consciousness, which means that since media play so large a role in our lives, the media help shape our consciousness.

Perhaps what extreme individualists like Margaret Thatcher are really arguing is that society may exist but that it is irrelevant. Many people probably agree with her. They can say this, but if they spend nine hours a day immersed in the mass media, which require all kinds of social, economic, political, and media institutions to create and disseminate their texts, the argument sounds a bit hollow. It is important that we keep this insight in mind—that we are all, as Durkheim put it, dual creatures and that we are in society and society is in us—as we investigate mass media and its role in society, because the same thing applies to it: The media are in society and society is, in many different and important ways, in the media.

The average American spends 9.2 hours each day using consumer media. More households report having video game equipment (62%), than having a subscription to a daily newspaper (50%). Of those U.S. homes with children, 70% own video game systems. Per day, children spend 59 minutes reading a book; 52 minutes using a home computer; and 45 minutes playing video games. 18% of teenagers 13–17 read "often," 50% read "sometimes," and 32% never read. American children who have home video games play with them about 90 minutes a day. Teenagers spend an average of 2.5 weekday hours on a home computer . . . 66% of U.S. children have a television set in their bedrooms. Children spend about 28 hours per week watching television. Over the course of a year, this is twice as much time as they spend in school. . . . Teenage boys spend nearly twice as much time watching MTV as reading for pleasure.

—"Popular Culture and the American Child"
site on World Wide Web

McLuhan became frustrated trying to teach first year students in required courses how to read English poetry, and began using the technique of analyzing the front page of newspapers, comic strips, ads, and the like as poems. . . . This new approach to the study of popular culture and popular art forms led to his first move towards new media and communication and eventually resulted in his first book, *The Mechanical Bride,* which some consider to be one of the founding documents of early cultural studies. While the *Bride* was not initially a success, it introduced one aspect of McLuhan's basic method— using poetic methods of analysis in a quasi-poetic style to analyze popular cultural phenomena—in short, assuming such cultural productions to be another type of poem. (2001: 4–5)

—Donald Theall,
The Virtual Marshall McLuhan

2

MEDIA USAGE IN
THE UNITED STATES

The figures in the quotation that opens this chapter give us a
pretty good idea of media usage in the United States. The fact
that 32 percent of American teenagers never read and that only 50
percent "sometimes" read is quite disturbing, since it is reading that
is all important in developing the critical thinking skills connected
both to individual social mobility and to participating intelligently in
the political process. Those who don't read become captives of the
kinds of media that require little intellectual effort—listening to the
radio, watching television, listening to CDs, watching films, and
playing video games.

Let me isolate the figures to give a better notion of how much
time children spend with certain media in a typical day:

240 minutes	watching television
59 minutes	reading a book
2 minutes	using a home computer
45 minutes	playing video games

We can see that we spend a great deal of time, each day, using consumer media. The question we must ask is—what effect, if any, does this use of consumer media have upon us as individuals and upon our society?

THE MEDIA WE USE

Let me list here the media we use in a typical day. I am using the term *media* in the way it is traditionally used—*as something that carries some kind of communication*. **Communication** involves sending messages from one or more senders to one or more receivers who can decode or understand the message that has been sent. The media not only *carry* "texts" (the term used in scholarly discourse for films, television shows, songs, and works of all kinds) they also *affect* these texts in different ways. The most common media are, then:

our voices	computers
our bodies	newspapers
telephones of all kinds	magazines
television	books
radio	billboards
recordings	photographs
films	videos

This list can be broken down in several different ways. For example, we could classify media according to whether they are essentially linguistic (using language) or photographic (using such things as images, facial expressions, gestures, and body language).

Communication theorists tell us that in a typical conversation, 70 or 80 percent of the information is generated by our facial expressions, body language, and other forms of **nonverbal communication.** But in some media, such as television programs and films, for example, we find both verbal and nonverbal communication techniques being used to generate messages, so that classification, while interesting, can be improved upon. I will say more about different ways of classifying the media shortly, after a primer on communication.

A PRIMER ON COMMUNICATION

The mass media are, more technically speaking, the mass media of communication. We can distinguish between different levels of communication and see where **mass communication** and the mass media belong:

intrapersonal	internal dialogue (talking to oneself)
interpersonal	talking to one person or a few people
small group	communicating with a small group of people
mass communication	using media to communicate with many people

There are many different models and theories of communication. Let me offer two classic and influential ones, which will give you a pretty good idea of how scholars see the communication process working. The first will be that of Roman Jakobson, a linguist, who said there are six elements in any speech act (see figure 2.1).

```
                          Content

                          Message

    Sender——————————————————————————————Receiver

                          Contact (medium used)

                          Code
```

Figure 2.1   Roman Jakobson's Six Elements of Communication

Let me explain each of these items in more detail.

- A *Sender*   sends (creates)
- A *Message*   the content of the communication (texts)
- A *Receiver*   the object of the message (audiences)
- A *Code*   the way the message is packaged (for example, in English)
- A *Contact*   the medium used (such as conversation or TV)
- A *Context*   which helps us understand the message better (society)

The *sender* can be one person, as in a conversation, or a group of people (as in a film or television show); the *message* can be words that contain information, or a combination of words and sounds and images; the *receiver* can be one individual or a million, who may be seeing a film or watching a television show; the *code* is the way the message is presented—in a language or by using words, images and sound, as in films or television programs; the *contact* is the medium used to send the message, and the *context* is the situation in which the message is sent, which helps determine its meaning. For example, the words "pass the hypodermic needle" mean something different if the context is a dark alley or a hospital.

Jakobson's model of communication offers us an insight into the people involved in communication and the way they communicate. It is one of the most famous and most useful models. Let me mention one other model (traditionally a **model** is defined as an abstract representation of what occurs in the real world), a very famous one offered by a political scientist, Harold Lasswell, in 1948. Lasswell asks:

Who?
Says what?
In which channel?
To whom?
With what effect?

Actually, this model by Lasswell is very similar to Jakobson's, as table 2.1 shows.

Table 2.1   Lasswell and Jakobson Models Compared

Lasswell	Jakobson
Who	Sender
Says	Code
What	Message
In which channel	Contact (medium)
To whom	Receiver
With what effect	

Jakobson's model doesn't deal with effects, the way Lasswell's model does; but there are, we can see, some similarities. Interestingly enough, Lasswell's **theory** has been criticized for bringing in the matter of effects, since **communications** scholars are divided on the matter of whether the mass media have long-lasting and important effects.

TRADITIONAL WAYS OF CLASSIFYING THE MEDIA

Now that we have an understanding of the process of communication, let me discuss the matter of how to classify the media. A commonly used classification breaks the mass media down into electronic, print, and photographic. This gives us the information shown in table 2.2.

Some media theorists link electronic media and photographic media into a hybrid they call photoelectronic media. If we use that concept, columns one and three would be merged. As a rule, we spend a great deal more time with electronic media and photographic media than we do with print media. The average person in the United States watches around 4 hours of television a day, which

Table 2.2   Ways of Classifying Media

Electronic Media	Print Media	Photographic Media
telephone	books	photographs
television	magazines	films
radio	newspapers	videos
recordings	billboards	

means television is the dominant medium in America (and in many other countries as well) followed by radio and listening to music on CD-ROMs and other new technology devices that can store many hours of songs. Americans don't, as the statistics on media use show, spend much time with print media, relatively speaking.

McLUHAN'S HOT AND COOL MEDIA

The late Canadian media theorist Marshall McLuhan used a different approach and classified media according to whether they were "hot" or "cool." He argued, in a famous aphorism, "the medium is the message." That is, the medium is more important than the textual content that the medium carries. While the medium has an important impact on the content it carries, McLuhan's notion that the medium is basic in the communication process—because it alters our sense ratios and modes of perception—is not generally accepted. His theories about hot and cool media, however, are worth considering in some detail.

According to McLuhan, hot media have high definition. By *definition,* he means that they are full of data, which leads to low participation. Cool media, on the other hand, have low definition, because they have little data and high participation.

As McLuhan writes in *Understanding Media:*

> There is a basic principle that distinguishes a hot medium like radio from a cool one like the telephone, or a hot medium like the movie from a cool one like TV. A hot medium is one that extends one single sense in "high definition." High definition is the state of being well filled with data. A photograph is visually "high definition." A cartoon is "low definition," simply because very little visual information is

provided. Telephone is a cool medium, or one of low definition, because the ear is given a meager amount of information. And speech is a cool medium of low definition, because so little is given and so much has to be filled in by the listener. On the other hand, hot media do not leave so much to be filled in or completed by the audience. Naturally, therefore, a hot medium like the radio has very different effects on the user from a cool medium like the telephone. (1956: 22, 23)

This passage offers McLuhan's reasoning behind his classification of media into "hot" and "cool" ones. His discussion of the work that audiences must do to make sense of cool media anticipates some of the thinking of scholars who talk about "reader-response" theory and the role an active audience plays in decoding texts in all media; these topics are discussed later in this book.

Table 2.3 offers examples of McLuhan's hot and cool media in paired oppositions.

We have to be more active in making sense of (or to use a communication theory term, "decoding") the texts carried by cool media. They invite our participation more than hot media do, because hot media supply a great deal of information and there's less for us to do. For example, radio conveys more information than a phone call does, and a photograph has much more information in it than a cartoon does.

McLuhan also speculated on the difference between print media and electronic media. There are, he suggests, certain logical implications that are connected to each kind of media. Print suggests linearity (we read lines of type, typically), logic, rationality, and

Table 2.3   McLuhan's Hot and Cool Media

Hot Media	Cool Media
radio	telephone
movie	television show
photograph	cartoon
printed words	speech
books	dialogues
lectures	seminars

Figure 2.2   According to McLuhan, a book is a "hot" medium and a cell phone is a "cool" medium. Hot media provide the user with more information.

connectedness. Electronic media, on the other hand, are associated with what might be described as "all-at-once-ness" and emotion. Table 2.4 is a comparison of McLuhan's notions about these two kinds of media.

I have taken these oppositions from McLuhan's writings—in particular, from his book *Understanding Media*. They reflect the intellectual, social, and political implications that stem from what McLuhan argued are the essential nature of the two different kinds of media.

It is possible to see how McLuhan derives linear thinking and individuality from books. When we read a book, we read letters that form words that form sentences that are printed, generally speaking, in horizontal lines of type. And books are read by individuals, who move through them at their own pace. So we can see how individu-

Table 2.4   Print and Electronic Media Compared

Print	*Electronic Media*
the eye	the ear
linearity	all-at-once-ness
interconnectedness	simultaneity
logical thinking	emotional responses
rationality	mythic spheres
books	radio
individualism	community
detachment	involvement
separation	connection
data classification	pattern recognition

alism and separation and detachment might be connected to the book. Electronic media are much different—they are often consumed by groups. They can be heard by individuals but also by groups, and thus they tend to bring people together instead of separating them, the way books do. The realm of sound involves, McLuhan suggests, pattern recognition rather than data classification, and this brings us much closer together into communities and thus closer to the realm of ritual and the mythic than print does. So a change in the popularity of a medium leads to other important changes in society, changes that ultimately have an impact on individuals, since we are all social beings.

McLuhan's ideas were very popular for several years, and he became a media celebrity. Then his theories came under attack by many communications scholars, and he faded from sight. Recently, however, McLuhan has been making a comeback, partly because media scholars see a connection between his theories of hot and cool media, for example, and the new digital technologies. His theories might help explain the current "passion" people have for using cell phones, for example.

THE MEDIA HELP SHAPE
THE TEXTS THEY CARRY

What many communications scholars don't deal with in their theories is the fact that we don't watch television, per se. We don't watch television . . . except when the screens go blank and we stare at the blank screen like dummies, waiting for the program we were watching to resume. The media always carry texts of one kind or another—news shows, sitcoms, sports programs, commercials, and so on. And due to the power of the media to profoundly influence the sounds we hear and images we watch, by editing and other manipulations, the medium does more than just transport texts. This notion that the media just transport texts is often known as the transportation theory of the media. This theory suggests that the media are relatively inert, an idea that is not generally accepted today.

Most media theorists believe that the media have an important role in shaping the texts they carry. In television, for example, the shots a director uses—zooming in, quick cutting, fading out, and so on—all of these shape our perception of what is happening in the texts we are watching. Think, for example, of the difference between watching a football game in a stadium and watching the same game on television, where the director can show a given play from three or four different camera angles, where he can zoom in on a player, where there are shots from blimps hovering above the stadium in which the game is being played. This matter of the power of a medium to shape the texts it carries is dealt with in some detail in my chapter on media aesthetics, which follows.

Everyday media experiences are not usually at the level of a major aesthetic experience, but for many persons *the most moving* cultural experience will be through popular media rather than classical art. A powerful emotional experience can be triggered by an otherwise trivial song floating out an alley and awakening rich associations. The important quality in the aesthetic experience, whether it is an emotional, earthshaking, life-changing encounter or a quiet, simple, weightless sense of deep appreciation is *your subjective response.* Seeing a captivating movie, hearing the right popular song at the right time, interacting electronically at maximum capability, getting caught up in a popular novel's sweeping narrative—these are sources of aesthetic experience shorn of artistic pretentiousness. By inspiring such moments, media culture can take on exceptional power, meaning, and importance. (1996: 13)

—Michael R. Real, *Exploring*
Media Culture: A Guide

During the Iran-Contra hearings that made Oliver North a national celebrity, Democrats learned what it meant to "lose control of the pictures." Steven Spielberg, the Hollywood director, was visiting Washington during the televised hearings. As he watched the hearings with some Democratic congressmen, he offered them a lesson in camera angles. "Watch this," Spielberg said, as he turned down the sound and directed the congressmen's attention to North's image on the screen. "The camera on North is shooting up, from about four inches below his eyes. This is the way they shot Gary Cooper in the western, *High Noon,* to make him look like a hero." When the camera panned to the committee members questioning North, Spielberg pointed out, the lighting was dim. Seen at a distance, they looked sinister. "It doesn't matter what Oliver North says. He has already won the battle, because he looks like the hero and everyone else looks like the villain." This realization shocked the congressmen. (1993: 13)

—Kiku Adatto, *Picture Perfect:*
The Art and Artifice of Public Image Making

3

THE SOCIAL DIMENSION
OF MEDIA AESTHETICS

To understand why mass mediated violence or any other kind of mass mediated programming works on its audiences the way it does, we must understand something about **media aesthetics.** *Aesthetics* is generally defined as a branch of philosophy involved in the study of beauty; but media aesthetics, as I will use the term, involves analyzing how creative artists use the technical capacities of the various media to achieve the effects they want. The term *aesthetics* has to do with sense perceptions, and so our concern is with how film and television and other media shape these perceptions. Media aesthetics deals, then, with how artistic effects are achieved, and these effects, I believe, play an important role in making a text meaningful to audiences. As the quotation from Kiku Adatto shows, things that we seldom think about or are aware of—like camera angles—can be very important.

I will be focusing attention mostly on television, but there is an aesthetic dimension to all media. Even in live theater, where performers have only their voices, facial expressions, and body language to use, we find directors using lighting, sound, costuming, action, and settings to create effects.

It is important for us to recognize that how a text is edited to clarify and intensify its message often has a social, economic, and political significance. For our purposes here, how a story is told is as revealing as what is told. Thus, for example, the way a political commercial is edited plays an important role in getting the message across. Style in fashion, we recognize, often has social and often political content; we can say the same about the aesthetic aspects of mass mediated texts. We begin this study of media aesthetics with a brief discussion of semiotics, the science of signs.

SAUSSURE ON SIGNS

How do we find meaning in things? How do we know how to interpret a particular facial expression or hairstyle? These questions are actually quite difficult, but there is a discipline devoted to exploring how we find answers to such questions—it is called semiotics, the science of signs. The term **semiotics** comes from the Greek word for sign, *sēmeîon*. A **sign** can be defined as anything that can be used to stand for something else. Thus, for example, a frown generally signifies or stands for the fact that one is unpleased. The term *tree* stands for a large, leafy plant.

One of the founding fathers of semiotics, the Swiss linguist Ferdinand de Saussure, said that signs were composed of two components: a *signifier* (a sound or object) and a *signified* (a **concept** or idea). He wrote:

> I propose to retain the word sign [*signe*] to designate the whole and to replace concept and sound-image respectively by *signified* [*signifié*] and *signifier* [*signifiant*]; the last two terms have the advantage of indicating the opposition that separates them from each other and from the whole of which they are parts. (1966: 67)

The relationship between the signifier and signified is arbitrary, based on convention. For example, there is nothing natural or logical in the relation between the word *tree* and the large, leafy plant that we call a tree. It could easily have been called something else. Words, then, are signs that stand for things, but there are many other kinds of signs.

Saussure wrote, in his book *Course in General Linguistics* (1966):

Language is a system of signs that express ideas, and is therefore comparable to a system of writing, the alphabet of deaf-mutes, symbolic rites, polite formulas, military signals, etc. But it is the most important of these systems.

A *science that studies the life of signs within society* is conceivable; it would be a part of social psychology and consequently of general psychology. I shall call it *semiology* (from Greek *sēmeîon,* "sign"). Semiology would show what constitutes signs, what laws govern them.

This may be considered one of the charter statements of semiotics. Saussure called his science semiology, but that term has been replaced by the term *semiotics* in recent years.

Saussure made another point that is very important. Concepts have meaning because of the web of relationships in which they are found; they don't have meaning by themselves. He wrote, "concepts are purely differential and defined not by their positive content but negatively by their relations with the other terms of the system" (1966: 117). He added that "the most precise characteristics" of these concepts "is in being what the others are not." What that means is that it isn't content, per se, that determines meaning, but *relationships* among the elements in a system. We make sense of concepts, then, by seeing them as the opposite of something else. Rich is the opposite of poor and weak is the opposite of strong.

For Saussure, nothing has meaning by itself, and the meaning of everything has to be learned. What this suggests is that we all have to learn media aesthetics, informally and on our own, as we watch films and television programs and play video games, if we are to understand everything that is going on in them.

PEIRCE ON ICONS, INDEXES, AND SYMBOLS

The other founding father of semiotics, who gave the science its name, was the American philosopher Charles Sanders Peirce (pronounced "purse"). He had a different theory than Saussure's, though both were interested in signs. Peirce said there were three kinds of signs: *icons,* which communicate by resemblance; *indexes,* which communicate by cause and effect; and *symbols,* which have to be learned. Table 3.1 shows these three kinds of signs.

We can see that there is a difference between Saussure's ideas about signs and Peirce's. For Peirce, only symbols are conventional and have to be learned. He once said, "the universe is perfused with signs, it is not composed exclusively of signs," which suggests that for Peirce semiotics is the key to finding meaning in anything.

We can combine Saussure and Peirce, and suggest that we find meaning in the world by seeing everything as either a signifier of something else (a signified—that is, a concept or idea) or as generating meaning by being iconic, indexical, or symbolic. We swim, like fish, in a sea of signs; everything is a sign, then, of something else. An **image,** for our purposes, can be defined as a visual sign or a collection of visual signs. In many cases, of course, we have signs within signs. For example, the White perfume advertisement shown here (figure 3.1) has two figures in it, two bottles of perfume, and words—so there are many smaller signs within the larger collection of signs that we can describe as an image. The expressions on the faces of the models, the clothes they are wearing, their ages, their body language, the jewels in the woman's belly button, the design of the ad, its lighting, and its color also function as signs.

LYING WITH SIGNS

One problem with signs is that they can be used to lie. As Umberto Eco, the distinguished semiotician and novelist, wrote:

> Semiotics is concerned with everything that can be taken as a sign. A
> sign is everything which can be taken as significantly substituting for

Table 3.1   Peirce's Three Kinds of Signs

Kind	ICON	INDEX	SYMBOL
Signify by	resemblance	cause/effect	convention
Examples	photographs	fire/smoke	flags
Process	can see	can figure out	must be taught

Figure 3.1 This perfume advertisement is filled with signs, from the expressions of the models to the design of the ad.

something else. This something else does not necessarily have to exist or to actually be somewhere at the moment in which a sign stands for it. Thus semiotics is in principle the discipline studying everything which can be used in order to lie. If something cannot be used to tell a lie, conversely it cannot be used to tell the truth; it cannot be used "to tell" at all. (1976: 7)

Bald men who wear wigs, brunettes who dye their hair blonde, malingerers who pretend to be ill—there are any number of examples of people lying, in varying degrees of seriousness, with signs. Eco's point is that if a sign can be used to tell the truth, it must also be able to be used to lie.

So, as I write this book, I pause for a moment and look out the window of my study. I see very tall plants (trees) and large objects (houses) with rectangular shapes in them (windows). When we are born, we know almost nothing. What we do, as we grow up, is learn a language or perhaps a number of languages. And what are languages—they are, simply put, composed of words (a kind of sign) that tell us what things are and rules that tell us how to use these words (grammar). We also unconsciously learn various **codes,** which can be defined as systems of signs and symbols that have meaning— one that is often not apparent. In espionage, codes are secret rules for unlocking the meaning in coded messages, but we can also think of codes in a cultural sense as being very similar to the codes spies use.

From a semiotic perspective, actors and actresses, if you think about it, lie with signs. They pretend to be certain characters who have certain emotions, which they express by such things as what they say, by the way they speak their lines, by their facial expressions, by their body language, and by the clothes they wear. We don't consider this kind of "lying" to be serious; in fact, we seek it out. We know what is going on with plays, films, and television shows, but are caught up in a temporary "willing suspension of disbelief," and so we become emotionally involved with what these performers are doing. When you move from the theater, from live performances, to mediated texts such as those found in videos, video games, television shows, and films, things become much more complicated. In the case of video games, for example, we are not merely spectators but actually become involved, interactively, in the story; and our actions can affect its outcome.

EDITING TECHNIQUES AND SEMIOTICS

When we consider texts in visual media such as film and television, we are dealing with works in which editing, different kinds of camera shots, lighting, music, and sound effects play an important role— perhaps, in some cases, a more important one than the dialogue spoken by the performers. It is useful to apply Saussure's distinction between *signifiers* (sound–image) and *signifieds* (concept, meaning) to different kinds of camera shots, camera movements, and editing techniques. Different camera shots and editing techniques function as signs, or cues to viewers—cues that tell them what to think and feel, and these cues are based on aesthetic codes people learn while watching television and films. Editing, for our purposes, will be considered to be the sequencing of different kinds of camera shots to create a sense of continuity in a text and generate certain desired effects. These camera shots and editing techniques are used with other matters such as sound, music, color, and lighting.

Camera Shot (signifier)	Definition of Shot	Meaning (signified)
establishing shot	large overview	location
close-up	head and shoulders	intimacy
extreme close-up	part of face	inspection
medium shot	head and torso	personal relations
full shot	complete body of person	social ambiance
long shot	setting and people	context, scope
extreme long shot	person in wider context	orientation
z-axis	vertical action from screen	involvement

As we grow up and become used to watching television, we learn the meanings of the various camera shots. We may not be able to

Figure 3.2   This print advertisement uses an extreme close-up photograph to attract attention.

articulate these meanings, but we get a sense of what the shot means. If we move to camera work, we find other meanings of interest.

Camera Movement	Definition	Meaning for Viewer
pans down	camera looks down on	power and authority
pans up	camera looks up to	weakness, smallness
dollies in	camera moves in	interest, observation
dollies out	camera moves out	scope, context
zooms in	lens moves in on	detail, focus
zooms out	lens moves out from	scope, context
arcs	semicircular movement	investigation
trucks left/right	horizontal movement	different perspective

Now I will deal with some of the more important transitional editing techniques that are conventionally used. These techniques enable editors to move from one image to another. The cut is the most commonly used editing technique, but others are available:

Signifier	Definition	Signified
fade in	black to image	beginning
fade out	image to black	ending
cut	switch from one image	simultaneity
wipe	screen image replaced by other	imposed ending
dissolve	image dissolves into next	weak ending

We can see, then, that there are many possibilities that directors and editors can use in shooting a text, and I haven't covered all of the different things that can be done in postproduction to a text. In some commercials, there is an incredible amount of quick cutting—some of them can have as many as sixty different images in a thirty-second commercial. So editing is an important element of the mass mediated arts.

We should think of the use of different kinds of shots and editing techniques as "instructions" to viewers to think certain things or have certain emotions. The order of images conveys meaning to viewers in the same way that the order of words does, and these meanings often have a social as well as a psychological dimension to them.

Editing involves the way media makers use different kinds of shots and different kinds of camera work to create the effects they want. As viewers watch a television program, for example, their ideas and emotions are affected not just by the words the characters utter and their actions but also by the different shots and combinations of shots and by the lighting, the sound, the music, and the colors used, among other things. I will now list and briefly discuss some of the techniques, mentioned above, that directors and production artists can do to intensify the meanings of texts.

Color

Colors have culturally important meanings to people, meanings that differ from country to country. We know, for example, that black means a certain thing in the United States and something different in other countries. Villains in American cowboy films were conventionally dressed in black and heroes were dressed in white.

Lighting

Lighting is an important cue for us about what is happening in a dramatic text. If the lighting is dark, we are in the realm of mystery and, in some cases, horror. Bright lighting, on the other hand, means something quite different and is associated with less dramatic entertainment genres.

Music

Music is used to help viewers of films and television programs connect, emotionally, to what is being shown on the screen. Music offers cues to audiences and helps them understand better what they are seeing, and it gives them cues that help them anticipate what might be coming. It establishes the emotional mood that the filmmakers want to generate and connects to the pace or rhythm of the images being shown.

Sound Effects

Sound also plays a role in giving audiences a better idea of what is going on in a text, and it helps intensify their experiences. We live in a world of sound and it is only natural that films, television programs, and video games (and all audiovisual texts) use the sounds that we are used to so as to make their texts seem more realistic. As we grow up we learn what certain sounds mean, so using sounds is a way of conveying information to audiences about how they should feel or what they might expect when they are watching a text.

THE NATURE OF NARRATIVES: VLADIMIR PROPP

A large percentage of the texts people watch on television and see at the movies are narratives—that is, stories. Stories have two axes: a linear or *syntagmatic* one, which involves one action following another sequentially (like words in a sentence or links in a chain) in time, and a horizontal or *paradigmatic* one, in which actions and characters take their meaning the way concepts do—by differentiation—that is, by being the opposite of something else.

Linear Axis	**Horizontal Axis**
Propp	Lévi-Strauss
syntagmatic	paradigmatic
sequence	relations
meaning from place in story	meaning from sets of oppositions

There have been many different attempts to understand how texts generate meaning as their plots develop sequentially. One of the most influential theories was developed by a Russian folklorist, Vladimir Propp. He said the most important thing to deal with in narratives are the actions of the characters, which he called "functions." He listed thirty-one functions that he found in Russian fairy tales, but that we can find (with minor modifications and updating necessary) in contemporary narratives—from fairy tales to James Bond films.

Propp's thirty-one functions are listed below. (Note: The initial situation is not considered to be a function.) These functions frequently are paired, and there is a logical nature, based on how the mind works, to the way they are used in narrative texts. Propp believed that the sequence of events in narrative was invariable, but we don't need to accept Propp's idea about the invariability of sequences of events to benefit from his analysis of narrative texts.

	Initial Situation	*Members of family introduced, Hero introduced*
1.	Absentation	One of the members of the family absents self.
2.	Interdiction	Interdiction addressed to hero. (Can be reversed)
3.	Violation	Interdiction is violated.
4.	Reconnaissance	The villain makes attempt to get information.

5.	Delivery	The villain gets information about his victim.
6.	Trickery	The villain tries to deceive his victim.
7.	Complicity	Victim is deceived.
8.	Villainy	Villain causes harm to a member of a family.
8a.	Lack	Member of family lacks something, desires something.
9.	Mediation	Misfortune made known. Hero dispatched.
10.	Counteraction	Hero (Seeker) agrees to counteraction.
11.	Departure	Hero leaves home.
12.	1st Donor Function	Hero tested, receives magical agent or helper.
13.	Hero's Reaction	Hero reacts to agent or donor.
14.	Receipt of Agent	Hero acquires use of magical agent.
15.	Spatial Change	Hero led to object of search.
16.	Struggle	Hero and villain join in direct combat.
17.	Branding	Hero is branded.
18.	Victory	Villain is defeated.
19.	Liquidation	Initial misfortune or lack is liquidated.
20.	Return	Hero returns.
21.	Pursuit, Chase	Hero is pursued.
22.	Rescue	Hero rescued from pursuit.
23.	Unrecognized Arrival	Hero, unrecognized, arrives home or elsewhere.
24.	Unfounded Claims	False hero presents unfounded claims.
25.	Difficult Task	Difficult task is proposed to hero.
26.	Solution	The task is resolved.
27.	Recognition	The hero is recognized.
28.	Exposure	The false hero or villain is exposed.
29.	Transfiguration	The hero is given a new appearance.
30.	Punishment	The villain is punished.
31.	Wedding	The hero is married, ascends the throne.

Propp also believed that there are only two kinds of heroes: *victim* heroes (who suffer from some action) and *seeker* heroes (who are sent on missions to accomplish something). In stories with victim heroes (and heroines), the focus is on how they are victimized and how they end their victimization. In stories with seeker heroes and heroines, the focus is on the way they help others who have suffered from some kind of villainy or are in danger. [To avoid the awkward nature of writing heroes and heroines all the time, I will use the term *heroes* to stand for males and females henceforth.] Seeker heroes often have helpers who aid them in various ways—they often have special powers or they give heroes some kind of magic agent that enables them to prevail over villains.

A PROPPIAN ANALYSIS OF JAMES BOND FILMS

Propp argued that all heroes are either seeker heroes or victim heroes. Quite obviously, many of the heroes in contemporary narratives are involved with rectifying some victimization that they or some member of their family have undergone, or are sent on missions to accomplish some goal. In some cases, we have a combination—such as the James Bond novels and films, where he is sent on missions to accomplish some goal. In some Bond novels, for example *Dr. No*, agents belonging to the British Secret Service (his "family") have been killed, so James Bond functions both as a hero from a "victimized" family or organization and a seeker hero.

The spymaster, M, sends Bond to Jamaica to find out what is going on; while there, he undertakes a hazardous mission to explore a small island controlled by a mysterious character, Dr. No. He is captured by the villain, Dr. No (an example here of personal victimization), and must undergo an ordeal of escaping from his confinement, during which time his life is continually threatened, so he can kill Dr. No (who had a mad plan to conquer the world) and end up in bed with Honeychile Rider, a beautiful woman he has befriended (the moral equivalent of marrying the princess). She is introduced in a chapter titled "The Elegant Venus." The Bond novels and films, then, can be seen as updated versions of fairy tales. We can find many Proppian functions in them, though in modernized versions and not in the rigid order Propp thought all narratives had to obey. (We can do the same for many television shows and films, and it might be an interesting exercise to use Propp's list of functions to analyze some contemporary film or television show.)

This particular Bond novel had negative portrayals of people of color, in particular black people and Asians, leading many critics to describe the book as racist. In recent years, we have become increasingly aware of the role the media play in giving people of color, women, ethnic minorities, gays, and other groups negative stereotypes that have destructive effects upon them. This use of negative stereotyping continues to be a problem with the media. Writers use stereotypes because doing so enables them to "explain," quickly and easily, why characters act the way they do.

THE NATURE OF NARRATIVES: CLAUDE LÉVI-STRAUSS

Propp's theory of looking at the order of actions or events in a narrative is known as syntagmatic analysis. A *syntagm* is a chain, so Propp's analysis looks at the chain of functions he believed all stories must have. Syntagmatic analysis tells us what happens in a text; but to understand the deeper or hidden meaning of the events in a text we must apply a different theory, based on the work of the French anthropologist Claude Lévi-Strauss.

Lévi-Strauss's theory is known as paradigmatic analysis, and is based on Saussure's notion that concepts don't mean anything in themselves. I quoted him earlier to the effect that "concepts are purely differential" and "in language there are only differences." We can extend this notion of concepts to include heroes and villains and their actions in narrative texts.

Lévi-Strauss is known as a structuralist; that is, he was interested in how the elements in something—a myth or a story—related to one another. The literary critic Jonathan Culler has explained (1976: 15) that structuralists take "the binary opposition as a fundamental operation of the human mind basic to the production of meaning." We make sense of things in general, then, by fitting them into sets of polar oppositions that our mind supplies to us. And we make sense of texts by seeing every action and every character in terms of the binary oppositions that exist in all texts—oppositions whose meaning we all know. Our minds are like computers when they decode texts, instantly providing us with oppositions that enable us to make sense of what is going on in a text at all times.

It is possible to see some of Propp's functions in terms of oppositions between heroes and villains, the two main characters in narratives. What follows in table 3.2 are very general oppositions that aren't always the case in every text, of course.

You can see from table 3.2 that many important oppositions can be found in narratives; and this list is only suggestive. We are continually setting up oppositions in our mind's "eye" as we read a book or see a movie or television program between the characters, events, objects, and so on that we see and their imagined or real opposites—that is how we find meaning in texts, and by extension, everyday life. It's quite easy, for example, to apply these oppositions to the various *Star Wars* films, James Bond films, and most films, as a matter of fact.

While many of these villains are evil individuals, criminals, and monsters of one sort or another, they have a social significance beyond the role they play in a particular text. The triumph of the hero over these characters confirms our sense that there is justice in the world and that good must inevitably triumph over evil, thereby

Table 3.2   Oppositions in Propp's Functions

HEROES	VILLAINS
young (sons)	old (fathers)
handsome	ugly (often grotesque and monstrous)
love	lust
heroines (rescued by hero)	enchantresses (bewitch heroes)
seeming villainesses	false heroines
imagination, invention	technology, manpower
seeks something	hinders hero
suffers from villain's acts	punishes hero
is dispatched	engages in reconnaissance
gets helpers (magic powers)	has henchmen
undergoes ordeals	creates ordeals
defeats villains	loses to hero

reinforcing our belief in goodness and the value of democratic institutions. Thus, when James Bond defeats the monstrous Dr. No,
Bond's victory is both personal and political. There are, of course,
many texts that are overtly political, such as the television shows
about the White House (*The West Wing*) and the Supreme Court
and, when elections come around, the numerous political commercials that are broadcast on radio and television.

Narratives are important in more ways than we might imagine.
As Laurel Richardson writes:

> Narrative is the primary way through which humans organize their
> experiences into temporally meaningful episodes. . . . Narrative is
> both a mode of reasoning *and* a mode of representation. People can
> "apprehend" the world narratively and people can "tell" about the
> world narratively. According to Jerome Bruner . . . narrative reason-
> ing is one of the two basic and universal human cognition modes.
> The other mode is the logico-scientific . . . the logico-scientific mode
> looks for universal truth conditions, whereas the narrative mode looks
> for particular connections between events. Explanation in the narra-
> tive mode is contextually embedded, whereas the logico-scientific

explanation is extracted from spatial and temporal events. Both modes
are "rational" ways of making meaning. (1990: 118)

So narratives are more than entertainments. They are a means by
which we seek to make sense of the world, both to ourselves and to
others. This means that the stories you read, the television shows you
watch, the films you see, the songs you listen to, the comics you read,
the video games you play, the jokes people tell you, and every other
narrative that you experience, play an important role in your consciousness and the development of your identity. Your "story" (by
which I mean your identity) is, in a sense, a story you build out of all
the other stories you know and to which you have been exposed.

One thing that this investigation of narratives reveals is that
members of audiences are much more active than we might imagine.
They have to interpret the meaning of every shot and sequence of
shots they see; they have to interpret the meaning of the camera
work; they have to make sense of the lighting, the music, and the
sound. They also have to find meaning in what the characters in a
text look like, what they say, what they do, and so on. In short,
there's a great deal that we must do every time we read a passage in
a book or see a film or television program or video. Of course we
have a lot of practice and experience doing this kind of work.

POSTMODERNISM AND MEDIA
AESTHETICS

There is a great deal of controversy about what postmodernism is and
isn't, and its influence on society and culture in the United States and
elsewhere. Scholars suggest that the movement known as **modernism** lost favor around 1960 and was replaced by **postmodernism**—a philosophical system which argues that the old philosophical
beliefs that used to guide people—such as a faith in progress and reason—no longer are valid. Some theorists have argued that postmodernism is really another name for the advanced form of capitalism
found in the United States and elsewhere. Sociologist Norman Denzin describes the postmodern sensibility, as reflected in the cinema

and television, in his book, *Images of Postmodern Society: Social Theory and Contemporary Cinema,* as follows:

> The ingredients of the postmodern self are given in three key cultural identities, those derived from the performances that define gender, social class, race and ethnicity. . . . These cultural identities are filtered through the personal troubles and the emotional experiences that flow from the individual's interactions with everyday life. These existential troubles look back to the dominant cultural themes of the postmodern era, including the cult of Eros, and its idealized conceptions of love and intimacy. The raw economic, racial, and sexual edges of contemporary life produce anxiety, alienation, a radical isolation from others, madness, violence, and insanity. Large cultural groupings (young women, the elderly, racial and ethnic minorities, gays and lesbians) are unable either to live out their ideological versions of the American dream or to experience personal happiness. They are victims of anhedonia, they are unable to experience pleasure. . . . They bear witness to an economy, a political ideology, and a popular culture which can never deliver the promised goods to their households. (1991: viii)

Among the films Denzin deals with in his study of postmodern film are *Blue Velvet, Wall Street, Crimes and Misdemeanors,* and *Sex, Lies, and Videotape.* Other writers have included such films as *Blade Runner* and *The Terminator,* amongst others, to this list. These postmodern films, videos, and television programs reflect with great power many of the problems that different groups of people—ethnic minorities, women, gays and lesbians—face in society, and the alienation they feel. These works also play a role in giving young people identities and belief systems. From the postmodern perspective, identities are flexible: You change your identity when you feel like it. The notion that identity involves something constant and unchanging is a modernist one; nowadays, you try on and cast off identities as often as you wish.

The postmodern sensibility can also be seen in television commercials that don't seem to mean anything and don't seem to convey a message (this applies to any number of perfume commercials) and in novels that don't come to a logical ending, such as Thomas Pynchon's *The Crying of Lot 49.* As a result of exposure to postmodern works, it has been suggested that contemporary youth now have a postmodern sensibility, which puts them at odds with older generations, which have a modernist perspective on things. What is called "generational conflict" is based not only on age, but on the difference between a modernist and postmodernist sensibility—one that is reflected in many of the films and television programs of the last forty years. (I will discuss other aspects of postmodernism, as it involves the relationship between elite and popular culture, in a later chapter.)

What media aesthetics attempts to do is determine, with some precision, how texts work and bring to consciousness the way individuals "decode" or make sense of these texts, hour after hour, day after day, without a second thought. It also is concerned with how aesthetic factors help shape text and consciousness. This is important if we wish to understand the social and cultural significance of images and of characters and their activities in narratives and other mass mediated texts of all kinds.

The place of the audience in the social structure makes a difference. Those who are well off are likely to be affected by a message about increases in taxation differently from those who are badly off.

An important factor has to do with **what the audience believes already**. Someone believing in self-sufficiency and independence will respond to an advertisement encouraging people to start up small businesses in a different way from somebody who believes in job protection and a job for life. **The greater the match between the views and knowledge of the audience and what is said in the communications, the more the communication will be believed.** (1990: 169)

—Graeme Burton, *More Than Meets the Eye:*
An Introduction to Media Studies

The critic may have access to a demographic profile of the audience, which includes the sociocultural categories that the audience members belong to: sexual identity, sexual orientation, religion, ethnicity, race, profession, educational level, income level, age, and political affiliation, to mention a few. The demographic profile will suggest a psychographic profile. . . . There are always individual differences and variations from the norm, but most public messages are designed to make sense to the largest possible audience, and they do. Even though Americans, for instance, may identify with very different cultural groups, they are exposed to many of the same messages via school, parents, and media, and therefore develop many of the same codes for making sense of messages. (p. 20)

—Jodi R. Cohen, *Communication Criticism:*
Developing Your Critical Powers

4

AUDIENCES I: CATEGORIES

In this chapter I deal with different categories of audiences. Individuals may not be aware of it, but media organizations have developed elaborate ways of classifying people into different categories—of interest to advertising agencies, who are trying to reach people to sell them goods and services. Each of us may think of ourselves as unique individuals, but for marketers our distinctive identities are of no concern—we're all, as far as they are concerned, members of some group or category based on demographics (our age, gender, race, religion, ethnicity), psychographics (values and beliefs), or something else.

AUDIENCES ARE SPECIALIZED

Audiences for many mass media texts are now global—think, for example, of audiences for American **popular** music, films, the broadcast of the Olympics and of the Super Bowl. In this chapter I will focus upon audiences in the United States, though what I write has applications to global audiences. We must remember, first of all, that audiences are part of a larger entity, namely the society (or societies, now that media are global) in which they are found.

In the United States, for example, we have a number of different and specialized audiences for the various kinds of radio shows: news, talk shows, sports broadcasts, and music shows, such as country western, classical, hard rock, light rock, rap, jazz, blues, and easy listening . . . I could go on and on. There are probably a dozen or more niche audiences for specific kinds of music on radio. That is why radio can be considered a **narrowcasting** medium—appealing, as a rule, to limited and very specific audiences, as contrasted with **broadcasting,** which aims for much larger audiences.

In many cases, people in what we can describe as micro-audiences are members of various **subcultures** that exist within the broader category of American **culture.** There are, for example, many different genres of video games, and video-game players can be broken down into which kind of console they use or whether they play video games on personal computers. And, audiences are much more active than we might imagine, both in the texts they select and the way they interpret these texts.

PROBLEMS ADVERTISERS FACE

Since radio and television commercials are sold on the basis of the size and characteristics of the audiences of specific shows, the radio

Figure 4.1   Video-game audiences can be subcategorized by the type of system or systems they use.

stations, television stations, and radio and television networks are interested in knowing how many people are listening to and watching their shows, and what these audiences are like. If you're selling a luxury car, it doesn't pay to advertise on a program mainly watched by viewers who cannot afford these cars. So advertisers have to pay careful attention to the programs on which they advertise.

The development of new technologies such as the TiVo digital video recorder, which enables people to record television programs and delete commercials, is causing all kinds of problems for advertisers. Some of them are dealing with this problem by increasing the use of product placements in shows—paying to have their products used in films and television programs, which is a kind of "stealth" approach to advertising. But product placement cannot solve the problem new technologies pose to the advertising industry and the companies for which the advertising agencies work. Just showing a bottle of soda pop isn't the same thing as having a commercial about it.

There is also the problem of clutter, in which viewers of television programs are assaulted by so many commercials that they forget what they have seen and get the commercials all mixed up in their head. As advertisers become more and more desperate to attract the attention of audiences by finding new and more fantastic images, they become involved in an ultimately self-defeating war for viewers. In addition, people quickly learn that the promises advertisers make are often spurious, and so audiences have become increasingly skeptical and increasingly difficult to reach.

SHARES AND RATINGS

Media researchers distinguish between ratings and shares when dealing with audiences. The difference between the two is explained in Barry L. Sherman's *Telecommunications Management: Broadcasting/Cable and the New Technologies*. Sherman writes:

> *Rating* refers to the percentage of people or households in an area tuned to a specific station, program, or network. For example, if, in a Nielsen sample of 1000 homes, 250 households were tuned to the ABC network, the rating for ABC during that time period would be (250 div 1000), or 25%. For ease of reporting, the percentage sign is

dropped in the ratings book. *Share* refers to the number of people or households tuned to a particular station, program or network corre- lated with sets in use. Continuing the above example, if only 750 of the sampled households were actually watching television in the time period covered, ABC's share would be (250 div 750) = 33%. Since there are always more sets in a market than there are sets in use, the share figure is always higher than the rating. (1995: 389)

These figures are important because radio and television networks are "selling" their audiences to advertisers, so a show with very high rat- ings and a high share (and the right kind of listeners and viewers) can charge much more for commercials than one with low ratings and a low share, or with the "wrong" kind of listeners and viewers. For example, the 2003 Super Bowl charged millions of dollars for each 30-second commercial because it knew it would have such a huge audience. Advertising works on a cost-per-thousand (CPM) basis, so a television show that is seen by hundreds of millions of people may actually cost less on a CPM basis than a show that doesn't charge very much, relatively speaking, but has a very small audience.

There is also the question of how reliable the various ratings sys- tems are. Nielsen, for example, asks people to keep a "Peoplemeter" for its national ratings. Sherman describes how Nielsen gets its data:

> The national Nielsens are produced through the use of the Nielsen Peoplemeter, a device resembling a cable box with a remote control. Over 4000 homes in the United States comprise a sample which, the- oretically at least, represents TV viewing in America's more than 94 million TV homes. The people meter is attached to each set in the participating household. Viewers push buttons assigned to them to track their viewing activity. The data are transmitted to the Nielsen Company and processed overnight so that ratings information can be used by programmers and advertisers by the beginning of business the following day. (1995: 383)

A sample size of four thousand people can get fairly accurate informa- tion about a television viewing population of 260 million people—if the sample is truly *representative* and if the people using the People- meter are diligent.

There are some questions about how representative the Nielsen sample is and how accurately the people using the Peoplemeters report their television viewing. The only way to be absolutely certain about television usage in America would be for all station changes to be recorded automatically in each household and for a camera to record how many people are in front of a given television set when it is on. Obviously, this is quite impossible. So we have to make do with statistical sampling, which while not perfect, yields quite accurate information, if done correctly.

We cannot separate media organizations that rely on the Nielsen ratings, such as radio networks, television and cable networks, and the marketing organizations that are so intimately connected with them. Advertising agencies have to choose certain programs on which to broadcast the commercials they produce, for example. So the broadcast media and marketing organizations are joined at the hip. Media broadcasting organizations and marketing organizations are, it is fair to say, different sides of the same coin.

In this chapter I will consider some of the different ways of breaking down the American market as being equivalent to segments of audiences in America. I will also use other typologies (classification systems) to distinguish between different ways of classifying audiences in America. We will start with **demographics,** which can be defined, broadly speaking, as the study of the social, economic, and other characteristics of human populations.

DEMOGRAPHICS AND AUDIENCES

Marketers classify audiences into a number of different demographic categories, based on distinguishing characteristics such as age, education, income, race, gender, ethnicity, marital status, and residence. Let me list some of the titles of books on marketing to different demographic groups that are found in a catalogue of marketing books I was sent a number of years ago (*Marketing Power: The Marketer's Reference Library*):

> *Wise Up to Teens*
> *Everybody Eats: Supermarket Consumers in the 1990s*
> *Kids as Customers*

Marketing To and Through Kids
Mature Americans: Myths and Markets
Hispanic Market Handbook
Mindstyles of the Affluent
Marketing to Women
Target the U.S. Asian Market

These groups are all "target audiences" that marketers try to reach, since members of these audiences presumably have special characteristics and purchasing patterns.

I will offer the blurbs for two of the books just listed. The first is *Wise Up to Teens: Insights into Marketing and Advertising to Teenagers,* by Peter Zollo:

> Here at last is the expert analysis that will help you capture your share of the nearly $100 billion that teenagers spend. This book explains where teenagers get their money, how and why they spend it, and what they think about themselves and the world around them. It presents five rules that will make your advertising more appealing to teens. Learn about brands teens think are cool, words to use in adver-

tising to teens, which media and promotions teens prefer, and how much influence teens have over what their parents buy. This is a fascinating look into the world of teens—a market whose income is almost all discretionary.

Zollo's book deals with an important demographic group for broadcasters and film studios—teenagers. It is probably somewhat of an exaggeration, but a large percentage of the movies that are made now have this segment of the American public (and teens in other countries, as well) in mind.

For my second example, let's consider the book *Target the U.S. Asian Market* by Angi Ma Wong, which is described in the following blurb:

> This book explains how to effectively reach the most affluent, well-educated, and fastest-growing consumer group in the nation—one that numbers over 7.3 million, with an impressive $225 billion in purchasing power. These consumers are a fascinating blend of centuries-old traditions and contemporary American culture. This marketing guide shows you where to get information: the impact of education and culture on the decision-making process; how to avoid potentially offensive intercultural mistakes; how numbers, colors, names, and *feng shui* affect your business; basic etiquette and much more.

We see, then, that for marketers, the United States is a collection of different demographic groups, each of which can be seen as an audience, each of which has particular characteristics, and each of which can be reached, so their decision making about purchasing products and services will be the way advertisers want this decision making to be—for the products and services they are selling.

As I suggested earlier, we all think about ourselves as discrete individuals, and, in one sense, in terms of our personal identity—our genetic makeup, our personalities, the way we look and think—we are. However, for marketers we don't exist as individuals; we are people who can be classified as members of various market segments and groups that theoretically can be "reached" by those who know, or work hard trying to figure out, how to "press the buttons" that motivate members of these groups, including each of us. In this respect, you might consider why it is that you buy certain brands of clothes, watch certain television shows, go to certain films, use certain shampoos, and eat certain foods—and the extent to which you have been, as advertisers would put it, "branded."

Consider, for example, what is available on the Asia Data Disk ($700) for marketers in Asia and for media outlets who want to know more about the people who take advantage of their services:

> Imagine presenting your Asian market overview, from scratch, in a day. This comprehensive reference product makes it easy for you to produce market reviews, new market assessments, and an overview of Asia's potential growth area. It allows you to analyze demographic and economic data for 14 Asian-Pacific countries from 1970 to 1994. You get 39 tables of information for each country. Variables include population by age and gender; educational attainment; spending for food, clothing, housing, furniture, health care, transportation, communications, recreation, and education; employment; real estate; GDP; exchange and interest rates; imports, exports, tourism, and ranking indexes.

What this means is that marketers and the media organizations that marketers use know a great deal about us, as far as our backgrounds (all of the variables just listed) and our purchasing powers are concerned—much more than we might imagine.

In addition to matters like age, race, and religion, some marketers look at audiences in other ways, such as considering the magazines they read. According to a survey conducted by one research company, Yankelovich and Partners, the magazines people read are a more valuable indication of consumer behavior than demographic factors. People, the authors of this study argue, choose magazines primarily based on their editorial content; and this editorial content is generally a reflection of their values, beliefs, and interests. The Yankelovich survey argues that people's behavior as consumers is coherent and logical. Their choice of magazines is an index, so to speak, to other choices they make as consumers.

It is useful for us to remember that the radio stations we choose to listen to and the television programs we choose to watch are also a form of consumption, though we may not think of it as such. And as the Yankelovich survey suggests, there is a connection between the media we consume and our other kinds of consumption—namely goods and services advertised in the media.

Marketers also look at groups based on their zip codes (that is, specific locations in cities) and the **lifestyles** that researchers have associated with these zip codes. For example, according to one marketing researcher, people who live in the 10021 zip code, in the Upper East Side of New York City, have a median income of $36,838; are liberal and moderate in their politics; have a "high use" of aperitifs, specialty wines, and champagne; and read *New York, the New York Times, Metropolitan Home,* and *Atlantic Monthly.*

What this means is that advertisers for companies that make and sell aperitifs, specialty wines, and champagne will look for the kinds of radio shows and television programs that people who live in the 10021 code most likely will listen to and watch. Our media, we must remember, are businesses. They must sell advertisements and commercials to audiences they attract in order to survive.

PSYCHOGRAPHICS AND AUDIENCES

Marketers and media researchers also break audiences down on the basis of **psychographics**—the psychological characteristics of audiences. Research organizations have come up with some interesting classification systems—that is, typologies—for various audience subgroupings based on whether members are "inner-directed" (think for themselves) or "outer-directed" (follow others) and categories like that. The psychographic marketing theorists suggest that values and beliefs are more important than demographic ones. Consumer motivations, psychographic marketers tell us, are not always identical to **socioeconomic** status and other demographic factors.

This means that people watch television programs, for example, because these shows reflect and reinforce their values and beliefs (which they may never have articulated or brought to consciousness) and are congruent with their lifestyles. People who watch *Joe Millionaire* and *Survivor* generally have different values and beliefs than people who watch *The News Hour with Jim Lehrer*. Thus, the psychographic theorists argue, the psychological profile of an audience can be more important than its age and income level. Let me offer, as an example, a well-known psychographic typology called VALS—for Values and Life Styles.

The VALS Typology

This **typology** or classification system was developed twenty years ago by SRI International, a think tank in Menlo Park, California. It focuses on people's lifestyles rather than on demographic statistics about them. The VALS 1 typology is based on theories of psychological development and divides audiences into nine different and distinctive kinds of people. The VALS typology has been modified over the years, but I will focus on the original system here. Breaking the market down into nine categories of consumers is important, SRI suggests, because advertisers can target their appeals to the specific values of each kind of consumer, or, for our purposes, members of each kind of audience.

This description of the VALS 1 typology uses material from articles by Niles Howard (*Dun's Review*, August 1981) and Laurie Itow (*San Francisco Sunday Examiner and Chronicle*, June 27, 1982). In her article, Itow explains the VALS system as follows:

> The system, called Value and Life-styles Program (VALS) draws on behavioral science to categorize consumers, not only by demographics such as age, sex, and the products they use, but according to their state of mind. Marie Spengler, VALS director at SRI, says the program is based on an analysis of cultural trends that can be used to develop products and target markets as well as match employees with jobs and make long-range business decisions such as where to build plants.

Categories of Consumers

VALS, Spengler says, captures "a deep, underlying sense of what motivates the consumer," using data from a thirty-question survey. Consumers are questioned about demographics, such as age and sex.

But more importantly, they're also asked about their **attitudes** and **values.** This gives SRI the data needed to create the various categories of consumers found in VALS. For our purposes, in this discussion of audiences, we can think of each of these categories of consumers as a segment of the more general American audience. The nine categories of consumers in the VALS typology are as follows.

NEED-DRIVEN

These consumers are "money restricted" and have a hard time just affording their basic needs. They are divided into two subcategories:

1. *Survivors* These people are old, poor, and out of the cultural mainstream.
2. *Sustainers* They are young, crafty, and on the edge of poverty but want to get ahead in the world. Need-driven consumers make up approximately 11 percent of the adult population.

OUTER-DIRECTED

These consumers, who often live in middle America, want others to feel positive about them. Outer-directed consumers make up close to two-thirds of the adult population in America, so if you're advertising something for mainstream Americans, the appeals should be for outer-directed types. There are three subcategories of outer-directed consumers:

3. *Belongers* They are conservative and conventional in their tastes, nostalgic, sentimental, and not experimental.
4. *Emulators* These people are upwardly mobile, status conscious, competitive, and distrustful of the establishment. They want to make it big.
5. *Achievers* They are the leaders of society, who have been successful in the professions, in business, and in the government. They have status, comfort, fame, and materialistic values.

INNER-DIRECTED

These consumers tend to purchase products to meet their inner needs rather than thinking about the opinions of other people. There are three subcategories of inner-directed consumers:

6. *I-am-me's* They are young, narcissistic, exhibitionist, inventive, impulsive, and strongly individualistic.
7. *Experientals* This group is in essence an older version of the I-am-me's and is concerned with inner growth and naturalism.

8. *Societally conscious individuals* They believe in simple living and smallness of scale, and support causes like environmentalism, consumerism (not the same thing as consumption), and conservation. This group made up around 28 percent of the adult population in 1990 and has, perhaps, grown considerably since then.

INTEGRATEDS

9. *Integrateds* This is the last subcategory, one that is characterized by psychological maturity, tolerance, assuredness, and a self-actualizing philosophy. These people tend to ignore advertising, and relatively few advertisements are made to appeal to them. Integrateds make up only around 2 percent of the adult American population, but they are very influential and are disproportionately found among corporate and national leaders. While integrateds may not be as susceptible to advertising as other groups, their taste in lifestyle products may be highly influential and they may function as what might be described as "taste opinion leaders."

This typology, which focuses on kinds of consumers, can also be thought of as listing micro-audiences, segments of the larger audience that are different from one another based on their values and beliefs and the way these values and beliefs are expressed in consuming products and services—but also, I would suggest, in "consuming" media. We can think of the programs the media carry as "products" to be consumed by segments of the American public, or other publics and audiences in other countries in certain cases. As you read over this list of VALS categories, you might want to consider which one of them applies to you, to your friends, to your parents, and to other people you know.

POLITICAL CULTURES AS AUDIENCES

The late Aaron Wildavsky, an extremely influential political scientist who taught at the University of California for many years, developed a way of breaking down democratic societies into four discrete **political cultures.** In an unpublished paper he wrote, "Conditions for a Pluralist Democracy or Cultural Pluralism Means More than One Political Culture in a Country," Wildavsky explained how he derived his political culture:

> What matters to people is how they should live with other people. The great questions of social life are "Who am I?" (To what kind of a group do I belong) and "What should I do?" (Are there many or few prescriptions I am expected to obey?). Groups are strong or weak according to whether they have boundaries separating them from others. Decisions are taken either for the group as a whole (strong boundaries) or for individuals or families (weak boundaries). Prescriptions are few or many indicating the individual internalizes a large or a small number of behavioral norms to which he or she is bound. By combining boundaries with prescriptions . . . the most general answers to the questions of social life can be combined to form four different political cultures. (1982: 7)

There are, then, two basic questions: *Who am I?* (does the group I belong to have strong or weak boundaries) and *What should I do?* (does the group I belong to have few or many prescriptions or rules). These two questions lead to four political cultures, based on whether the boundaries are strong or weak and the number of rules is few or many.

The four political cultures are, Wildavsky suggested:

fatalists	prescriptions numerous, group boundaries weak
individualists	prescriptions few, group boundaries weak
elitists	prescriptions numerous, groups boundaries strong
egalitarians	prescriptions few, group boundaries strong

Fatalists think they are victims of bad luck and are apolitical; individualists stress the importance of limited government, which should do little more than protect private property, and believe in free competition; elitists believe that stratification in society is necessary but also have a sense of obligation toward those below them, unlike the individualists; egalitarians emphasize that everyone has certain needs that must be taken care of (especially the downtrodden fatalists) and tend to oppose mainstream political thought in America.

According to Wildavsky, you need all four groups for democracy to flourish in a country, and the four groups need one another. He saw the individualists and elitists as being the dominant groups in America and the egalitarians as the loyal opposition. People in America may not recognize that they belong to one of these political cultures, or be able to articulate the beliefs of a given political culture. The matter is further complicated because people sometimes move from one group to another, except for the fatalists, who are stuck down at the bottom of the totem pole and seldom have the chance to rise.

If you think about it, each of these four political cultures also represents a kind of audience for books, radio shows, television programs, films, and other media. I used to play a learning game with my students when I taught courses on media and **popular culture** in which we looked at these groups as audiences. One premise we used is that people seek *reinforcement* in the media for their basic beliefs and values and wish to avoid **cognitive dissonance.** Thus they will watch television programs that affirm and support the values they believe (that provide reinforcement) and avoid ones that attack their values and beliefs (and generate cognitive dissonance). Table 4.1, adapted and updated from one of our game-playing sessions a number of years ago, offers an example of the four political cultures as audiences.

From this table, I think you can see how it might be that members of different political cultures, with different core values and beliefs, might choose to read certain books, watch certain films, and decide on who to vote for in elections. These four audiences may not always have articulated their beliefs to themselves or others, and they may not be conscious of what motivates them, but it can be seen that in many cases there is a logic to the choices members of audiences make as far as consuming media is concerned. It seems rather obvious that people who watch *Sex in the City* or *Alias* are probably quite different from those who watch *Nova* or *Nature.*

Table 4.1   Political Cultures and Popular Culture

TEXT	ELITIST	INDIVIDUALIST	EGALITARIAN	FATALIST
Books	The Prince	Looking Out for Number One	I'm Okay, You're Okay	1984
Films	Top Gun	Color of Money	Woodstock	Rambo
TV Shows	News Hour	Survivor	American Idol	Smack Down Wrestling
Songs	God Save the Queen	I Did It My Way	We Are the World	Anarchy in the UK
Sports	Polo	Tennis	Frisbee	Roller Derby
Games	Chess	Monopoly	New Games	Russian Roulette

What complicates matters is that in some cases an individual who is a member of one political culture (for example, individualist) may be thinking of moving to another one (for example, elitist). That means their media choice could be based on the change the person is thinking of making in political cultures rather than on reinforcing the political culture to which he or she belongs.

ACTIVE AUDIENCES: DECODING MASS MEDIATED TEXTS

In recent years, media scholars have begun to recognize that members of audiences are more active than we thought they were. When the **hypodermic needle theory of the media** was popular, and we believed that everyone got exactly the same message from a mass mediated text, the role members of an audience (from one individual watching a television show to the huge numbers of people who are watching that show) played was not considered important.

Now, however, the hypodermic theory has been abandoned and replaced by what might be described as **reader response theory** or sometimes as **reception theory,** which is the opposite of the hypodermic theory. Wolfgang Iser, a leading advocate of reader-response theory, explains his thinking as follows:

The text as such offers different "schematized views" through which the subject matter of the work can come to light, but the actual bringing of light is an action of *Konkretisation*. If this is so, then the literary work has two poles, which we might call the artistic and the aesthetic: the artistic refers to the text created by the author, and the aesthetic to the realization accomplished by the reader. From this polarity it follows that the literary work cannot be completely identical with the text, or with the realization of the text, but in fact must lie halfway between the two. The work is more than the text, for the text only takes life when it is realized and furthermore the realization is by no means independent of the individual disposition of the reader— though this in turn is acted upon by the different patterns of the text. (1988: 212)

Iser is talking about literary works, but we can extend the notion of a literary work to cover any text carried by the mass media. Everyone who watches a mass mediated text interprets it on the basis of his or her temperament, education, background, and knowledge base.

For example, when we watch a television show, we bring to the process of watching that show our culturally shaped knowledge base that enables us to make sense of what we are watching. This involves applying the aesthetic "codes" that we've picked up as we grew up watching television, our knowledge of rules of behavior, our understanding of spoken language and body language, and any number of other things. That is, we are always decoding the texts we see on television.

In the case of a novel, for example, according to Iser, a novel without a reader is inert; it takes a reader to bring a novel to life, and readers play an important part in interpreting novels and other kinds of mass mediated texts. At the very least, in the case of films and television shows, audiences have to interpret visual phenomena, sound effects, and dialogue.

Iser's approach may seem a bit extreme, but it serves to point out the role audiences play in the scheme of things. They are not, at the very least, passive receivers of texts. We have to learn how to "read" television programs and films and all kinds of other texts in ways analogous to the way we read books. And where we are in the social structure, as Graeme Burton points out, also affects the way we read texts. All of these complications involved in interpreting texts suggest that the question we must ask when dealing with a film or television program or any other text is not whether our interpretation is right or wrong, but whether it is interesting and comprehensive—whether it reveals important matters found in the text and explains the power the text has over audiences.

That is, we all "read" texts based on our experiences in our societies and the "grid" that growing up in a given culture and time period imposes on our minds. This helps explain why works of art are so useful in understanding the society and culture in which they are produced—for that grid or schema is also, to varying degrees, in the mind of the creator of a given text. We can say that it doesn't make sense to argue whether the interpretation of a text is correct or incorrect. And taste is not important, for tastes vary and one might say that in a postmodern world, taste is irrelevant. You may or may not have liked *Kangaroo Jack* or *The Matrix,* but that's not important. What is important is the degree to which an interpretation explains what happens in the text and can relate it to social, psychological, and cultural concerns, thus providing a stimulating analysis.

ACTIVE AUDIENCES: USES AND GRATIFICATIONS

This notion, that there is often a logic to the choices people make in selecting one or another television program, for example, leads to my next topic—the uses people make of the television shows and films they watch, and the gratifications that these television shows and films (and by extension all kinds of other texts) provide. The **uses and gratifications** approach to audiences contrasts with the most commonly used approach, which focuses on the "effects" of media on individuals and groups of people, and society in general—the subject of the next chapter. Some argue that the uses and gratification concept is dated, but it seems important to me that we think about how people use mass mediated texts as well as how these texts use people.

Let me offer here a list of some of the more important uses and gratifications. This list was compiled from various sources and studies. I will separate uses and gratifications by assuming that *uses* involves matters essentially involving the relation of individuals to society and that *gratifications* refers primarily to psychological matters, though my separation of uses from gratifications is, admittedly, somewhat arbitrary.

Uses

1. To share experiences with others in some group or community.
2. To find models to imitate.
3. To help gain an identity and a personal style.
4. To obtain information about the world.
5. To affirm and support basic values.
6. To see order imposed upon the world.

Gratifications

1. To see authority figures deflated or exalted.
2. To experience beautiful things.

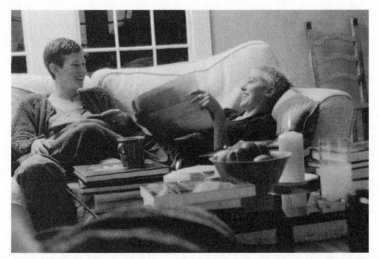

Figure 4.2 Keeping informed about world events is one reason people use media such as newspapers and books.

3. To identify with the divine.
4. To find diversions and distractions.
5. To empathize with others.
6. To experience extreme emotions in a guilt-free and controlled situation.
7. To reinforce a belief in the ultimate triumph of justice.
8. To reinforce a belief in romantic love.
9. To reinforce a belief in the magical, the marvelous, and the miraculous.
10. To see others make mistakes (and feel satisfaction in not having made those mistakes oneself).
11. To participate in history and events of historical significance in a vicarious manner.
12. To be purged of unpleasant feelings and emotions (a catharsis).
13. To obtain outlets for sexual drives in a guilt-free manner.
14. To explore taboo subjects with impunity and with no risk.
15. To experience the ugly and the grotesque.
16. To affirm moral, spiritual, and cultural values.
17. To see villains in action.

We must recognize that a given text might provide several different uses and gratifications and that different people will obtain different gratifications and make different uses of events in a given text. For example, viewers of talk shows might get information about how to deal with problems they face, gain information about topics of interest, see models they wish to imitate (such as guests on a show and their clothes, the way they talk, their "style," and so on).

These uses and gratifications come, in large measure, from surveys in which social scientists asked people (who, for our purposes, can be seen as members of audiences) questions like why they watch soap operas or what they get from listening to certain kinds of music. One problem with uses and gratifications is that it is difficult for researchers to determine, objectively, which uses and gratifications are generated by specific events in a given text, and it is difficult to quantify the results of this kind of research. Nevertheless, it seems pretty obvious that audiences are attracted to various specific mass mediated texts and genres of texts because there is some payoff for them, and these payoffs are the uses these texts can be put to and the gratifications they provide. That explains why huge numbers of people watched the final episode of *Joe Millionaire* and a long documentary about Michael Jackson that aired in February 2003.

Texts also have many different effects on people. This is a matter of great interest to media researchers and the subject of the next chapter.

The entire study of mass communication is based on the premise that the media have significant effects, yet there is little agreement on the nature and extent of these assumed effects. This uncertainty is the more surprising since everyday experience provides countless, if minor, examples of influence. We dress for the weather as forecast, buy something because of an advertisement, go to a film mentioned in a newspaper, react in countless ways to media news, to films, to music on the radio, and so on. There are many reported cases of negative media publicity concerning, for instance, food contamination or adulteration, leading to significant changes in food consumption behaviour. Our minds are full of media-derived information and impressions. We live in a world saturated by media sounds and images, where politics, government and business operate on the assumption that we know what is going on in the wider world. Few of us cannot think of some personal instance of gaining significant information or of forming an opinion because of the media. (1994: 327)

—Denis McQuail, *Mass Communication
Theory: An Introduction*

Nearly everything we do to enlarge our world, to make life more interesting, more varied, more exciting, more vivid, more "fabulous," more promising, in the long run has an opposite effect. In the extravagance of our expectations and in our ever increasing power, we transform elusive dreams into graspable images within which each of us can fit. By doing so we mark the boundaries of our world with a wall of mirrors. Our strenuous and elaborate efforts to enlarge experience have the unintended result of narrowing it. In frenetic quest for the unexpected, we end by finding only the unexpectedness we have planned for ourselves. We meet ourselves coming back. A Hollywood love triangle, according to Leo Rosten, consists of an actor, his wife, and himself. All of us are now entangled with ourselves. Everywhere we see ourselves in the mirror. (1975: 255)

—Daniel J. Boorstin, *The Image:
A Guide to Pseudo-Events in America*

5

AUDIENCES II: EFFECTS

I n this chapter I consider the effects of media on audiences. The media affect us on many levels: They give us ideas, they help shape our opinions and attitudes, they affect our emotions, they affect us physiologically, and they affect our behavior, among other things. But are these effects significant and are they long-lasting? Are the media doing things to us that may be harmful? Are the media doing anything socially constructive? Let me begin this chapter on media effects with a question that is at the heart of many of the criticisms of the mass media and mass culture.

IS MASS CULTURE MAKING
US ALL MORONS?

Some media theorists argue that the mass media and popular culture—sometimes combined into "mass mediated culture"—*must*
destroy the elite arts (by which I mean things like serious novels,
poetry, classical music, and plays) since Gresham's law suggests that
junk art always drives out good art. But this doesn't appear to have
come true. Let me cite some statistics about the book publishing
industry, for the year 2000, taken from www.bookwire.com.

Category	*Number of Books Published*
Arts	1073
Biography	3899
Business	4068
Education	3378
Fiction	14,617
History	7931
Juveniles	8690
Literature	3371
Philosophy	5556
Poetry, Drama	2479
Religion	6206
Science	8464
Sociology, Economics	14,908
Technology	8582
Travel	3170

We published 122,000 books in the United States in 2000, which
means that each day approximately 135 books were published. Each
day we published 41 books on sociology and economics, 40 works
of fiction, 23 science books, and 15 philosophy books. In 2000, the
book publishing industry was a $25 billion industry, larger than the
film industry and the video-game industry combined.

Many of these books are, no doubt, of poor quality—formulaic
romances, trashy novels, and so on. But we must remember that a
large percentage of books published in the elite genres—"serious"

novels, poems, plays, and so on—are also second- or third-rate works. In the final analysis it is the skills and abilities of the writers and artists, not the art forms they use, that count. A great writer like Dashiell Hammett can take a lowbrow genre like the tough-guy detective novel and turn it into a masterpiece like *The Maltese Falcon*.

It is reasonable to argue that popular taste is not, as a rule, elevated—and that has been the case for centuries. But this does not mean that a considerable amount of great art is not produced—for a relatively small percentage of the population, generally speaking— and it is unlikely that popular culture is driving out good art and rapidly moronizing us all . . . or even most of us.

JOHNNY AND TIFFANY MAKE DINNER

In this vignette, we find Johnny and Tiffany "multitasking," like so many people in America and other societies as well.

> Johnny and Tiffany are making dinner at her apartment before watching *Friends*. They are in the kitchen, but the television set, located in the living room, is turned on. Tiffany is washing lettuce and making a salad of lettuce, tomatoes, cucumbers, and avocados. Johnny is grilling hamburgers on a George Foreman electric grilling machine. They are both "listening" to the television program that is on and occasionally walking into the living room to glance at it. For dinner they have the salad Tiffany made, grilled hamburgers on buns, and frozen French Fried potatoes that Johnny zapped in the microwave. For dessert they have ice cream and coffee. After dinner they go into the living room. It is time for *Friends*. They think the show is "really cool."

Johnny and Tiffany are like millions of other people who do other things while they are "watching" television. The fact is, generally speaking, that people do not sit, hour after hour, with their eyes glued to the television set, but do a number of different things while their sets are on. Life goes on in front of the television set—people pet their dogs, go to the bathroom, chat with one another, go to the kitchen for snacks, read newspapers and magazines, and so on. So we

---

"Mass Marketing Climbs the Wall for Victory Lap"

The idea that something called "mass culture" would reduce the life of the mind to homogenized glop dates all the way back to at least the 18th century, when Germany's J. W. Goethe worried that the newest high-tech tool of his day, newspapers, would emulsify the world into group-think. . . . The threat didn't reach America in a way anyone would notice until sociologists in the 1950s started writing about masscult, conformism and men in gray flannel suits. . . .

Living with the reality of mass marketing has been one of the greatest love-hate relationships in all American history. European intellectuals tend simply to resent and hate it. Both leftists and conservatives consume it, all the while worrying that the more the mass market spreads, the more it flattens everything. . . .

The sense grows that one is everywhere being confronted, manipulated and pushed by someone's marketing campaign. Yet despite the torrent, no backlash has emerged like the beatniks of the '50s or the hippies of the '60s and '70s. We have the anti-global demonstrators, but they're obviously idiots. Where's the outrage?

It's nowhere, because the fact is that "Spider-Man" (the ultimate misfit) is really good. So is Sam Adams beer and Starbucks coffee, Callaway golf clubs, Pepsi, Prada, Krispy Kreme, Harry Potter, Barnes & Noble, Walgreens, the Discovery Channel, Levis, LensCrafters, Absolut, ESPN, Dominos and Diane Krall.

The mass market in America, the median of quality, has *risen,* not fallen. We may all be drinking from the same coffee cup and spending weekends together watching the same computerized movie graphics, but, as the saying goes, it's all good. The fears of corporatized conformity were overblown. East Germany was conformity. This is commercial anarchy born of competition.

Source: Daniel Henninger, *Wall Street Journal,* 10 May 2002, p. A10.

---

have to make a distinction between a television set being on and people watching it; not everyone watches television with undivided attention.

We must keep this in mind when we read about the number of hours people watch television and the effects television has on people. Television is part of their lives, and relatively small numbers of people give it all their attention. The boob tube is blaring away, but Johnny Q. Public and Tiffany Greatgal are multitasking. That is, they are doing several things at the same time. Like many people, they are just using television programs as a kind of background to their activities.

In the preceding chapter I dealt with different ways of classifying audiences, with some of the ways that members of audiences use the media, and with the gratifications they obtain from them. In this chapter, I take a different approach and consider the effects that the media *may* be having on members of audiences. Denis McQuail, in the quote at the beginning of this chapter, makes an important point: We all believe that the media have effects—or, more precisely, from my point of view, the texts carried by the media (and in part shaped by them) have effects. But we have a very hard time proving, to the satisfaction of scholarly researchers, that these mass mediated texts have long-term and important effects.

THE CONCEPT OF MEDIA EFFECTS NEEDS QUALIFICATION

I think it is somewhat of a simplification to talk about "media effects" when dealing with television since, as I have pointed out, we don't watch television per se but watch specific texts—programs broadcast on/carried by television (and other means such as cable and satellites). And the same, of course, applies to all media. Media researchers talk about media effects the way they do because they are looking for ways of dealing with large aggregates of people and texts, and so they simplify things and talk, for example, about the amount of violence on television (generally, on an hourly basis) or the way television portrays women (in commercials or in narratives or other genres).

This is perfectly understandable, but we should always remember that texts play an important role in providing a context for and characterizing events that take place in them—as the example "pass the hypodermic needle" (dark alley or hospital?) demonstrates.

I will focus my attention on television here, since it is the medium with which we spend the most time and is the most powerful of our daily media experiences. But what I say about television can be applied to movies, music videos, video games, and other media. Many of the texts we see on television are narratives of one sort or another—that is, they tell a story and have some kind of a beginning, some kind of conflict to be worked out or problem to be solved, and some kind of a resolution.

This is important because narratives have the power to move us and to affect us, in profound ways, emotionally and intellectually. I alluded to this in my discussion of the "vicious cycles" in television, earlier. We should also keep in mind that genres commonly not seen as narratives—such as commercials (which are often micro-dramas), sports programs, talk shows, and game shows—often have powerful narrative and dramatic components to them. Even news shows can be seen as being composed of little narratives that form a larger narrative.

With all these qualifications and caveats in mind, let me offer some of the most commonly held criticisms of the mass media and the popular culture texts they carry. I will be talking mainly about television, but many of the criticisms also apply to other media such as film, radio, magazines, newspapers, and popular music.

CRITICISMS OF THE MASS MEDIA
AND THE TEXTS THEY CARRY

I offer, here, some commonly made criticisms of our mass mediated texts, sometimes offered as attacks on the mass media in general and at other times as attacks on television, "the medium everyone loves to hate." All through history, members of various social, intellectual, and aesthetic elites have attacked the taste of the common people and made the kind of arguments I offer here.

You may find some of the attacks quite convincing, and you might consider others rather extreme. The important thing is to be aware of what many critics consider to be the numerous negative effects that come from spending the amount of time we do with the media, in general, and television, in particular. I will focus my attention on television because we watch it for around four hours each day; though, as I mentioned earlier, the arguments I make here about television (taken from a variety of sources) can also be made about other media.

1. Critical Faculties Overwhelmed

The argument here is that television "overwhelms" us. Due to the amount of television to which we are exposed as well as the power of this medium, we eventually and inevitably abandon our critical faculties and our capacity for clear thinking and rational decision making.

2. Desensitization to Violence

Because of all the violence to which viewers of television are exposed, they become desensitized to violence's real nature, leading to a lack of concern about violence and, perhaps, a tendency by some viewers to rely on violence in their own lives to "solve" problems. This desensitization to violence may also have an impact on our attitudes toward sexuality, since it can be argued that violence often has a psychosexual dimension.

3. Distorted Picture of Reality

Television doesn't show the world the way it really is, but offers a highly distorted picture. The world shown on television is full of violence and sexual innuendo; we watch countless killings and murders on television, but most people never see anyone killed or murdered in real life. The new so-called reality programs such as *Survivor, Big Brother,* and *Joe Millionaire* are frauds—they are highly edited and the people in them are not a cross section of the kind of people we deal with in our everyday lives. Many of the people we see on television are unusual. For example, the female models in commercials tend to be tall and exceedingly slim, and the men often are very handsome. Ethnic minorities, people of color, children, the elderly, and women are all underrepresented. We don't get a representative sampling of American society on television, by any means. The reality we find on television, we must remember, is always a mediated, highly edited, distorted image of reality.

4. Diverts Serious Creative Artists

Because television pays such incredible salaries, it "seduces" many serious writers, directors, and performers into working for it, diverting them from the theater and other elite art forms and depriving audiences for this kind of art of their contributions. (This was particularly true of the film industry, which used to hire stables of great writers to crank out film scripts.) The attractions of the media are so great that it is difficult for serious artists to resist, which means that fewer serious dramatic and literary works are created.

5. Escapism

Television provides essentially escapist fare—silly comedies, violence-ridden action adventure shows, and similar kinds of material

Figure 5.1   How "real" is reality TV? Participants on shows like *Survivor* usually aren't representative of the people we know or encounter every day.

with little redeeming social and aesthetic value. Because these shows don't deal with serious issues and are so superficial, people can consume enormous quantities of this material. There are some news shows, but even they have become dominated by the need to "entertain." Media critics have pointed out that there are relatively few television documentaries, dealing with serious issues, compared to twenty or thirty years ago.

6. False Consciousness Created

The stories shown on television tend to suggest that the so-called American Dream is alive and well and that anyone with enough determination and willpower can, inevitably, succeed. Most of the characters on television narratives tend to be middle-class or affluent people. This implies we live in a society that is classless in that it is, for all practical purposes, all middle class. Minorities, ethnic groups, and racial and other groups tend to be ignored, and the terrible difficulties people in the working classes face are seldom dealt with. Some critics of television argue that it should be seen as a subtle kind of brainwashing, meant to convince people to accept the status quo.

7. Formulaic Nature

To enable audiences to understand quickly what is going on in narratives, television scriptwriters use very conventional stereotyped characters and story lines. That is, television is very "formulaic" and avoids material that might be challenging because it is original and inventive and requires a certain amount of effort by viewers. Because watching television and films requires so little effort, many children and adolescents find it difficult to put in the effort required to read a book.

8. Fragmentation

The way a typical hour of television broadcasting is broken up, with numerous commercials and station promos, leads to a sense of life, in general, as fragmented and disorderly. The problem is often exacerbated because one frequently sees a large number of commercials for different products, one after another. Finally, in the course of an evening's viewing, one can see any number of different kinds or genres of programs: news, sitcoms, horror shows, and action adventure, which reinforces the sense of life as fragmentary. Postmodern theorists argue that the pastiche or hodgepodge (that is, a mixture of different styles and genres) is the dominant metaphor for understanding contemporary American culture, so it might be that our mass media both reflects and reinforces a postmodern sensibility.

9. Homogenization

The other side of the psychological fragmentation argument is that television, film, and American popular culture, in general, are spreading American culture all over the world (especially the Third World). This leads, it is held, to a destruction of these "weaker" native cultures and the dominance of American and First World culture and, ultimately, a kind of homogenization in which all cultures are more or less alike: watching American films, eating McDonald's hamburgers, drinking Starbucks espressos, and abandoning their native traditions and culture. Some critics argue further that our popular culture also spreads our capitalist ideology, which is hidden in the texts and not obvious to those who consume them.

10. Hyperactivity

Due to the rapid bombardment of images and the kind of instant gratification that television provides, there is reason to suspect that television viewing contributes to hyperactive behavior in many children. They are used to being endlessly amused and entertained and do not develop the ability to be quiet in classrooms and to concentrate on their studies. The incredible rise in the number of children (and now adults) diagnosed with attention deficit disorder or attention deficit hyperactivity disorder may be connected to high levels of television viewing and other kinds of media exposure.

11. Irresponsibility

The notion that the people who decide what to show on television are irresponsible and more interested in profit than the well-being of their audiences is an ethical one. The airwaves are owned by the public and, in principle, television and radio should further the public's well-being. Instead, in a mad quest for ratings, television producers broadcast a great deal of junk that has wide appeal but is harmful. For example, many of the commercials for beer are directed toward adolescent sensibilities and shown on programs that adolescents watch. This, critics assert, has led to a serious drinking problem in many young people—large percentages of whom we have recently discovered are binge drinkers.

12. Isolates People

Although television creates a huge audience of viewers, almost all of the people viewing television programs are isolated into little family groups. Statistic reveal that a large percentage of school-age children have their own television sets in their rooms, which means that the family is no longer a television viewing audience; it has been fractionated even at that level, and now children watch television shows in their own rooms. This argument ultimately suggests that television leads to increased alienation in people, who cut themselves off from others—even, sometimes, from members of their own families.

13. Lowest Common Denominator

This is one of the most commonly made attacks on television (and the mass media in general)—that it is aimed at the lowest common denominator. This means, it waters things down, oversimplifies things, avoids important issues—in an effort to please as many people as it can. In theory, the "lower" you go, the more people you'll attract, which implies that ultimately there are forces in motion to generate works that are moronic—such as the infamous celebrity boxing match with Tonya Harding and Paula Jones in March 2002. This show received very high ratings, supporting the "Gresham's

Law" notion of some critics that bad programming drives out good programming.

14. Manipulation

Television, it is asserted, manipulates its viewers by using humor, sexuality, and anything else it can to attract audiences and, in the form of commercials, tries to get people to purchase advertised products and services. In addition, because television shows only certain perspectives on news events, it manipulates public opinion. People say "seeing is believing" without thinking that when they watch television, someone always determines what they see—and that what they see may be taken out of context, or in scholarly jargon, decontextualized.

15. Narcotic

There is reason to suggest that television functions like a narcotic for some people, who become psychologically dependent on it and sometimes even describe themselves as "hooked" on it. That is, they become television addicts. Like many addicts, they lack an awareness of their addiction, seeing themselves as people who "like" television but can live without it. Some viewers develop *parasocial* relationships with certain characters they watch on television, and feel that they actually "know" these characters and the performers who play them. These viewers have a need to be with these characters on their favorite shows, which can be seen as a pathetic substitute for real-world relationships.

16. Obsession with Narrow Range of Topics

Television is obsessed with a relatively narrow range of topics— violence, sexuality, consumption, youth, celebrity, and a few others—from a vast number of topics relative to the human condition that it could deal with. Television executives argue, "we only give people what they want," neglecting the fact that all people in audiences can do is "select" from what it available on television, satellite, or cable that night. This narrowness of focus in television leads, ultimately, to a diminished sense of possibility in viewers and a constricted notion of what it means to be a human being. Television, it could be said, doesn't give people what they want but teaches them to want what they can get.

17. Passivity Induced

Watching television is a passive experience—one sits and watches. The only physical activity might be pressing a button and zapping a program or eating something. This television viewing experience is typically punctuated by trips to the bathroom and refrigerator. Because of all the television viewing that young people do, many of them are growing obese in alarming numbers. Obesity is now an epidemic in America. Thus, television watching has certain biological, as well as psychological, effects on members of audiences. And these biological changes have social implications, because obese people tend to suffer from many medical problems such as heart trouble and diabetes, leading to higher medical costs for everyone. With some young people we find an interesting situation—passivity, while watching television, and hyperactivity, when not watching television.

18. Privatism

The argument that television leads to privatism means that viewers of television learn to focus on their own lives and personal concerns and neglect social matters and the public realm, in general. We become distracted from serious matters—involving politics, decisions about social issues, and that kind of thing—and focus, instead, on our own concerns, in particular our desires for consumer products and services. Thus television viewing leads to materialism. We find, for example, many young people know very little about our history or anything else, in many cases; but they know everything about pop culture celebrities and have incredible "product knowledge" (learned from advertising). This privatism among the general public means that small groups that are politically motivated and organized exercise inordinate power over our social and political agenda. Large numbers of people do not vote in elections, because they are all wrapped up in themselves, so the argument goes, and can't be bothered with any-thing else—even though political decisions made by elected officials affect their lives in profound ways.

19. Sentimentalism

Television dramas are often criticized for being excessively senti-mental, for generally having "happy endings," for calling up more emotion than is necessary in the various kinds of narratives it broad-casts. That is, television tends to neglect the tragic dimensions of human life, washing everything over with a veneer of optimism and focusing it all through rose-colored glasses.

20. Sexploitation

The roles women are given in television dramas, and the way they are portrayed in television commercials and other texts, exploits their sexuality and uses them to create sexual excitement and sell products. Even though feminists have spent many years attacking the roles women are given in narratives and the way television exploits female sexuality, there has been little improvement. Women are not

---

What Students Know

According to a recent survey of America's most elite universities, nearly all college seniors could identify *Beavis and Butthead* but 40% could not place the Civil War in the right half-century. A national his-tory test of high-school seniors found a majority of them identifying Germany, Italy or Japan as a U.S. ally in World War II. Still another survey of Americans at large found a third attributing the line "from each according to his ability, to each according to his needs" to the Constitution rather than Karl Marx.

Source: The Wall Street Journal, 4 February 2003, p. W15.

portrayed in realistic ways, generally speaking; the focus is on their bodies and not on their minds, characters, or personalities.

It might be that there is so much vicarious sexuality available on television that the interest of viewers in real sexual activity becomes diminished, or that the erotic fantasies generated by television dominates their thinking, leading to negative feelings toward real-world partners.

21. Trendmaker

Interestingly enough, large numbers of Americans pride themselves on their individuality and uniqueness, on "doing their own thing." Yet, television has incredible power to create trends, fads, and crazes—usually involving matters like clothing styles, hairstyles, language use ("master of my domain"), and that kind of thing. It has been argued, then, perhaps carrying things to extremes, that we are a nation of sheep. Each of us has the illusion that we are different from others—even though we may look like everyone else and talk like everyone else—in our culture in general or in some subculture to which we belong. We are caught in a contradiction—we want to be ourselves, but we also aspire to be "trendy" or "with it."

22. Violence As a Solution

It has been suggested that many mass mediated narratives use violence as an easy "solution" to dramatic problems rather than using other methods. Much of what we know about the world is based on what is called "incidental learning," learning that we pick up out of the classroom, and it may be that what many people learn from these dramas, without being conscious of what they are learning, is that violence is the best way to deal with certain difficulties. Thus, all of a sudden, or so it seems, we read about all kinds of "rages" that have recently been identified, such as "road rage" and "flying rage."

There is evidence to suggest, now, that media organizations are cutting down somewhat on the amount of violence and sexploitation in the texts they carry. A survey made in 2002 shows a decrease in the amount of violence and sexuality in television—perhaps in response to all the negative publicity that media organizations have received about the violence and sexual exploitation in the media. But this decrease does not mean that there is not excessive use of violence and sexploitation on television, in films, and in many music videos.

With this, I bring to an end my discussion of numerous criticisms that commonly are made about the mass media—and especially television. I offer next a discussion of some extreme attacks on the media that have been made in earlier years—examples of what I call "anti-media rage."

ANTI-MEDIA RAGE

It is interesting to consider the vehemence with which the mass media have been attacked by some scholars—perhaps an example of what might be called anti-media rage? As an example, let me cite from the introduction by Bernard Rosenberg to a book he co-edited with David Manning White, *Mass Culture: The Popular Arts in America*—an important anthology on the media published in 1957. It is generally considered one of the first books to seriously examine the mass media and popular culture—now often called mass mediated culture. I have eliminated some phrases and similar material in the interest of economy, but offer Rosenberg's indictment in all its fury:

> People in mass cultures become *dehumanized, deadened, anxiety-ridden, exploited, entrapped, lonely, debased,* and their lives are *standardized, vulgarized* and *manipulated* by mass culture, which is a threat to our autonomy, and this situation is exacerbated by things such as *sleazy fiction, trashy films, bathetic soap operas,* creating, in the general public, *unrest, lives emptied of meaning and trivialized,* as well as *alienation* (from past, work, community and possibly one's self) leading to that horrendous entity, mass man. Mass culture is *cultural pap* and *gruel* that *cretinizes* our taste, *brutalizes* our senses (paving the way for totalitarianism), and destroys our taste so that all we like is *kitsch.* [My italics.]

Rosenberg, quite obviously, thinks that popular culture, the mass media, and mass culture are highly destructive of our well-being both as individuals and collectively as a society. He hypothesizes that it is mass culture, made possible by modern technology, that lies at the root of our problems—not our national character or our economic system. In essence, he is suggesting that mass culture is the logical and necessary result of the development of modern technology.

DEFENDERS OF THE MASS MEDIA
AND POPULAR CULTURE

Not everyone is as negative as Rosenberg, of course. His co-editor, David Manning White, offers a different and more positive assessment of television:

> Take, for example, the offerings of the television networks on Sunday, March 18, 1956, a Sunday which I chose at random. The televiewer would have been able to see on this day a discussion of the times and work of Toulouse-Lautrec by three prominent art critics; an inspiring interview with Dr. Paul Tillich, the noted theologian; a sensitive adaptation of Walter von Tilburg Clark's "Hook," a story of a hawk's life, a powerful documentary on mental illness with Orson Welles and Dr. William Menninger; an interview with the Secretary of Health, Welfare and Education; an interview with the Governor of Minnesota on the eve of the primary elections in his state; an hour and a half performance of *Taming of the Shrew* in color with Maurice Evans and Lilli Palmer. (1957: 18)

White points out that there is a lot of excellent programming on television, and adds that critics of mass culture "will invariably choose the mediocre and meretricious" to focus their attention on when they deal with the media and popular culture. In other words, their choices can be characterized as an example of **selective attention;** they neglect anything that is good and focus their attention and fury on anything that is mediocre or bad.

Let me offer an update, almost fifty years later, of what White did by telling what's on network television on Sunday, March 17, 2002, in San Francisco. I will focus on the kind of programming he cited in his report. Viewers in San Francisco could have watched:

- *Face the Nation, Meet the Press,* and other interview news programs.
- Member's Choice on the public television channel, Channel
  9, which was raising money. Various "special" shows were on
  all weekend featuring doo-wop groups and so on.
- *Snow White: The Fairest of Them All* (film)
- *Beyond the Prairie II: The True Story of Laura Ingalls Wilder* (film)
- *60 Minutes*
- *Simpsons*

The networks were full of basketball games ("March Madness"), sitcoms, game shows, and so on—not the heady fare of the fifties that
White listed. Of course many people now have cable and can get
movies and other kinds of shows, so my list of network shows may
not be representative of what's on television—including satellite television and cable television, and people now have videocassette players and DVD players, so what's on the network isn't the whole story,
by any means. And March 17, 2002, was not a representative evening—because CBS was broadcasting the college basketball playoffs
and the public television channel was having a pledge drive.

There are, it is fair to say, many scholars who defend television
and the mass media on several different fronts. I will deal with some
of these defenses in the following section.

OTHER DEFENSES OF THE MASS MEDIA
AND THE TEXTS THEY CARRY

Defenders of the mass media, mass mediated culture, and popular
culture (or, for our purposes, the texts carried by the mass media)
have some points to offer regarding the attacks made by critics of the
media, and some arguments to make on their own behalf. I once
wrote an article titled, "Why Is Popular Culture So Unpopular?" My
point in the article was that popular culture was very popular with
the masses of people for whom it was created; however, it was
unpopular with academics, scholars, and various elites, who argue
that most popular culture is junk (which is generally true) and its
effects have generally been very harmful (which is debatable).

Figure 5.2   We spend much of our lives consuming mass media, but experts disagree on how this activity affects us.

William McGuire, a psychologist at Yale University, has offered the following assessment of what might be called the debate over television and the mass media, in general. His essay, "Who's Afraid of the Big Bad Media?" discusses research on a variety of subjects related to media effects, such as indoctrination and **social control.** McGuire writes:

> Evidence in support of the claim that the media have sizable direct impact on the public is weak as regards each of the dozen most often-mentioned intended or unintended effects of the media. The most commonly mentioned intended effects include: (1) the influence of commercial advertising on buying behavior; (2) the impact of mass media political campaigns on voting; (3) public service announcements' efficacy in promoting beneficial behavior; (4) the role of prolonged multimedia campaigns in changing lifestyles; (5) monolithic indoctrination effects on ideology; and (6) the effects of mass-mediated ritual displays on maintaining social control. The most often cited unintended effects of the mass media include: (1) the impact of program violence on viewers' antisocial aggression; (2) representation

in the media as a determinant of social visibility; (3) biased presentation of media as influencing the public's stereotyping of groups; (4)
effects of erotic materials on objectionable sexual behavior; (5) modes
of media presentation as affecting cognitive styles; and (6) the impact
of introducing new media on public thought processes. (Berger,
1991: 274)

McGuire argues that there is little evidence that the media have the
effects they are held to have by critics. Thus, many of the criticisms
found in the earlier section on effects can be attacked as being speculative and theoretical, and perhaps ideological—that is, not based on
empirical evidence—or as involving short-lived and relatively limited
phenomena.

Defenders of television and the mass media also suggest, like
David Manning White, that it has brought millions of people ballet,
opera, serious drama, and other works of so-called elite culture—
works they never would have seen otherwise. Thus, the mass media
have, on balance, positive effects for their audiences. This assertion
that television has brought culture to the masses is correct, but I
would counter that the amount of "culture" is minimal contrasted
with the amount of third-rate material available.

I would suggest that now the dominant view among researchers
is that most of the evidence available leads to the notion that media
effects are not weak and limited, but powerful. For example, as a col-
league of mine, Chaim Eyal, has written:

> The limited effects notions are conceptualizations of the past. Very
> few, if any, theoreticians cling to those ideas. In the first place, the
> notion of null, or limited, effects originated from a very narrow line
> of research—the impact of political campaigns, studies in the late
> 1940s and early 1950s. Not much later it was recognized effects are
> not only in the realm of behavior but also in the area of cognition:
> awareness, knowledge, opinions, etc. With this recognition, which
> paralleled the development of the concept of attitudes by social psy-
> chologists, came the recognition that the mass media do have an
> impact—indeed different types of impact—in specific areas of peo-
> ple's thoughts, information processing and life in general. (personal
> communication, 1999)

So there is reason to believe that the effects of television and the mass media are not as limited and minor as defenders of the mass media argue.

THE POSTMODERN SOLUTION

Earlier I discussed postmodernism with a focus on the way it is reflected in films. I pointed out that postmodern society is characterized by a lack of adherence to overarching philosophical systems and beliefs. The phrase that Jean-François Lyotard, a French scholar, used to characterize postmodernism in *The Postmodern Condition: A Report on Knowledge* is "incredulity toward metanarratives." In postmodern societies, people no longer accept the old philosophical systems that used to justify their beliefs and actions.

Eclecticism and the pastiche become the dominant metaphors for postmodern societies. People can have multiple identities, which means they can, at different times, be members of many different audiences. As Lyotard explains:

> Eclecticism is the degree zero of contemporary general culture: one listens to reggae, watches a western, eats McDonald's food for lunch

and local cuisine for dinner, wears Paris perfume in Tokyo and "retro" clothes in Hong Kong; knowledge is a matter for TV games. (1984: 76)

That is, an individual can have multiple identities and consume many different kinds of culture in the course of a day or week.

One significant thing about postmodern thought is that it breaks down the barrier between elite culture and popular culture. In essence, postmodernists argue, elite culture and popular culture aren't that different, and in many cases it is hard to tell the difference between them. Take, for example, an Andy Warhol painting of a comic strip hero, Dick Tracy. Is that elite culture or popular culture? So for postmodernists, there is just culture; and different kinds of culture appeal to different groups, subcultures, media audiences, or interpretive communities within society.

As Douglas Kellner writes in "Postmodernism as Social Theory: Some Challenges and Problems":

> As opposed to the seriousness of "high modernism," postmodernism exhibited a new insouciance, a new playfulness, and a new eclecticism embodied above all in Andy Warhol's "pop art" but also manifested in celebrations of Las Vegas architecture, found objects, happenings, Nam June Paik's video-installations, underground film, and the novels of Thomas Pynchon. In opposition to the well-wrought, formally sophisticated, and aesthetically demanding modernist art, postmodernist art was fragmentary and eclectic, mixing forms from "high culture" and "popular culture," subverting aesthetic boundaries and expanding the domain of art to encompass the images of advertising, the kaleidoscopic mosaics of television, the experiences of the post holocaust nuclear age, and an always proliferating consumer capitalism. The moral seriousness of high modernism was replaced by irony, pastiche, cynicism, commercialism, and in some cases downright nihilism. (1988: 239)

Thus, it can be argued that postmodernist thought cuts the Gordian knot created by the tangled and complicated debate over elite and popular culture, by slicing through the barrier that critics had used to separate them. If popular culture and elite culture are more or less the same, as the postmodernists argue, then the debate over the effects of popular culture and the mass media becomes irrelevant.

If I may be allowed a historical analogy: the technically advanced societies are at a point in their history similar to that of the emergence of an urban, merchant culture in the midst of feudal society in the Middle Ages. At that point practices of the exchange of commodities required individuals to act and speak in new ways, ways drastically different from the aristocratic code of honor with its face-to-face encounters based on trust for one's word and its hierarchical bonds of interdependency: Interacting with total strangers, sometimes at great distances, the merchants required written documents guaranteeing spoken promises and an "arm's length distance" attitude even when face-to-face with the other, so as to afford a "space" for calculations of self interest. A new identity was constructed, gradually and in a most circuitous path to be sure, among the merchants, in which a coherent, stable sense of individuality was grounded in independent, cognitive abilities. . . . In the 20th century, electronic media are supporting an equally profound transformation of cultural identity. Telephone, radio, film, television, the computer and now their integration as "multimedia" reconfigure words, sound and images so as to cultivate new configurations of individuality. (1998: 255, 256)

—Mark Poster, "Postmodern Virtualities," in
Arthur Asa Berger (ed.), *The Postmodern Presence*

Technocultures are awash in tools. Generally considered the most important of the cybernetic tools, the computer is actually more of a workbench, or desktop, upon which one works with one's tools. The word processors, nonlinear digital video editing systems, database managers, Web server softwares, interactive multimedia programs, and even esoterica like virtual reality "world-building" kits are what constitute the tool commodities of the technoculture. These commodities are not simply consumed; instead, they produce new commodities and new work.

—Peter Lunenfeld, *Snap to Grid: A User's*
Guide to Digital Arts, Media, and Cultures

6

THE SOCIAL IMPACT OF NEW
MEDIA TECHNOLOGIES

We tend to think of the new media technologies that are developing so rapidly now in terms of their primary functions, which involve entertainment or communication. The impact of these new technologies on these areas has been incredible. But these new media technologies also are having important social, economic, cultural, and political consequences, as Mark Poster, quoted earlier, suggests. Most people are aware that American culture and society are changing (and the rest of the world, as well) as the new technologies start making their impact felt; but we don't, as a rule, appreciate the incredible impact these new technologies are having on American culture and society.

For example, large numbers of people now have cell phones, which are very convenient and useful in many different circumstances. But some cell phone users, who make terrible nuisances of themselves, conduct the most intimate conversations, often in a loud voice, anywhere they happen to be—in restaurants, in airport lounges, and even in toilets. Cell phones now ring in the middle of plays, at symphony concerts, in school lecture halls, and while religious services are being conducted. Often this happens because people forget to turn their phones off, but not always. Some people consider it vital to be accessible at all times and don't care whether they disturb other people. Interestingly enough, many people now

99

consider it chic *not* to be reachable by cell phone—that is, they wish to guard their privacy and limit their accessibility to others. Cell phones used to be signifiers of importance, but are now so common they have lost their cachet.

In this chapter I deal with the "social" impact, in the broadest sense of the term *social,* of the new media technologies on American culture in society, and consider such topics as computers and the Internet, the development of virtual communities, the video-game phenomenon, and new video and audio recording and playing devices.

Consider what has happened to the medium of television as the result of new technologies. At one time we had only three national television networks and some local stations; now, countless cable and satellite channels are available to people who subscribe to them. Some people have lamented that now "we have 500 channels but there's nothing's on." By this they mean the same genres that were carried by television networks are now found on the cable networks, except that some cable outlets are now very specialized and carry programming devoted only to specific genres such as music videos, sports, news, old films, or comedy.

To understand what is happening in this brave new mass mediated, digital world we live in, we must understand what **digital** means. It is to that subject I now turn.

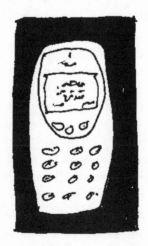

New Media Technologies and Teen Taste

Relatively recent developments in media technology, such as satellite transmission, the remote control, the VCR, and the Internet, have expanded enormously the number of media materials available and have given teens in the United States much more control over when and where they will use them. In the next five years, other technological innovations such as digital compression will bring an estimated three hundred program choices into most U.S. homes; by 2010 most homes will have a thousand channels or "content windows." . . . Other media, such as radio, magazines, and movies are already highly specialized and offer an array of content that appeals to a variety of tastes and interests. Today's teens have the opportunity to select their own media diets from a smorgasbord of possibilities.

Source: Jane D. Brown and Elizabeth M. Witherspoon, "The Mass Media and Health of Adolescents in the United States," in Y. R. Kamalipour and K. R. Rampal, *Media, Sex, Violence, and Drugs in the Global Village* (Lanham, Md.: Rowman & Littlefield, 2001), 78.

THE DIGITAL WORLD

The first thing we must come to grips with is that the new media technologies involve the replacement of analog technologies with digital ones. Consider the kind of watches everyone used to wear: They had a hand sweeping around the dial as the seconds passed, and they had a minutes hand and an hours hand. These watches were analog watches, based on the notion that things are connected to one another, that time is continuous, that we live in a world in which there are many degrees of difference. The word *analog* is very similar to the word *analogy*, which means "similar to something," or "like something."

In the digital world, everything is separated. With digital watches and clocks, time becomes a series of discrete moments, succeeding one another but not showing that any moment in time is related to any other one. With an analog watch, you can glance at your watch and say "it's a quarter to five," but with a digital watch you get a readout saying, in effect, it is now 4:45 p.m. and so many seconds.

Peter Lunenfeld, a scholar who has written several books on art and the net technologies, offers an excellent explanation of what the term *digital* means in his book, *The Digital Dialectic: New Essays on New Media*:

> Digital systems do not use continuously variable representational relationships. Instead, they translate all input into binary structures of 0s and 1s, which can then be stored, transferred, or manipulated at the level or numbers of "digits" (so called because etymologically, the word descends from the digits on our hand with which we count out those numbers). Thus a phone call on a digital system will be encoded as a series of these 0s and 1s and sent over the wires as binary information to be reinterpreted as speech on the other end. . . . It is the capacity of the electronic computer to encode a vast variety of information digitally that has given it such a central place within contemporary culture. As all manner of representational systems are recast as digital information, then all can be stored, accessed, and controlled by the same equipment. (1999: xv)

Lunenfeld offers the example of the digital photograph that is composed of a number of pixels, "a grid of cells that have precise numerical attributes associated with them, a series of steps rather than a continuous slope" (1999: xvi). The new media technologies are digital then, and are based on binary oppositions between various combinations of 0s and 1s—that is, ons and offs—and grids of separate cells with numerical attributes.

In the following list I present some important media and the date of their digitization.

Year	Medium
1962	Telephone
1967	Print
1977	Films (segments of *Star Wars*)
1995	Complete films (*Toy Story*)
1998	High definition television (HDTV)

We see, then, that we are in an age of digitalization and that our media are now almost completely digitized—with the exception of television, which is slowly becoming so.

THE COMPUTER AND CULTURE

In the early days, when computers were just being developed, one businessman—I think he was the head of IBM—suggested that the

Figure 6.1 The first computers sometimes filled large rooms. Today, portable computers can go almost everywhere we do—even to the beach.

entire United States could use, maybe, five computers. At that time, computers cost millions of dollars and filled up large rooms. Today, it isn't unusual to find families with five computers. Originally, people used computers because of so-called killer applications like spreadsheets and then word processing and, later, image manipulation. Now, of course, computers are ubiquitous and can be used to do all kinds of remarkable things.

The price of computers has gone down over the years. I bought my son a Commodore 64 (64K) for $900 around 1980, and $900 then was worth a lot more than it is worth now. In 2001 I bought my wife a new Hewlett-Packard computer with 256 MB of RAM, a 40-megabyte disk drive, a chip speed of 1.1 GHz, a 15-inch color monitor, loads of software, and an inexpensive inkjet printer—for $650. And the store where I purchased the computer gave me a year of free Internet service, worth approximately $250, which means the computer ended up costing around $400.

There is the matter of what has been called "the knowledge gap" to be considered. Those with access to computers and other new technologies quite obviously have an advantage over those who do not have access to them. In recent years, however, our schools and libraries have purchased computers, so they are more available than ever before. Nevertheless, many families at the bottom rungs of our socioeconomic ladder do not have the funds to purchase their own computers and to purchase access to the Internet, so children in these families are seriously disadvantaged.

With the development of the Internet, the computer now is seen as an important communication device, not just something that can be used for databases or spreadsheets or for word processing or manipulating images. Or, in recent years, for playing video games. People send billions of e-mail messages to one another, and are bothered by businesses sending them billions of undesired e-mail advertising messages (Spam). With the Internet, the world is open to us, but that also means we are open to the world and vulnerable to all kinds of people whom we will never meet and who don't know who we are—some of whom are criminals and others of whom are malicious.

The growth of the Internet also is changing our media usage behavior. There are now millions of websites that people visit, for one reason or another. Many companies use websites to sell products and services on the Internet. Many stores ("bricks") now also have elaborate websites where they sell their merchandise ("clicks").

The phenomenon of "cruising"—that is, looking around—the Internet is now worldwide, helped by powerful search engines such as Google and AltaVista. On a recent visit to Vietnam, for example, I noticed that the streets of downtown Hanoi were lined with video cafes that were full of tourists and Vietnamese sending e-mail and using the Internet for other purposes. I made use of these video cafes myself, to keep in touch with friends and my family. Many other cities all over the world now have video cafes.

The number of sites on the Internet and the subjects they deal with are astounding—everything from sites with online books to fan sites dealing with video games or movie stars, from sites dealing with abstruse and esoteric philosophical movements (Google lists 147,000 sites with something about postmodernism in them) to sites dealing with medical problems or selling books or cameras or groceries or whatever. In the San Francisco area, you can now buy groceries on the Internet; two supermarket chains—Safeway and Albertson's—deliver the order to your house for a fee.

Figure 6.2   Cybercafes, Internet cafes, and video cafes are found in many countries, providing access for people who don't own computers and allowing travelers to keep in touch with people back home.

The marriage of computers and printing devices has led to the development of digital printing presses that enable publishers to print books on demand and to print their covers and bind them. This "print-on-demand" phenomenon has the potential to revolutionize publishing. So the computer is having an incredible impact, not only on publishing and television, but in all kinds of other areas—from medical imaging to downloading music.

The darker side of the computer is that it enables governments to store information about people—and some communications theorists worry that the power of the government to gather and to store information about people can lead to all kinds of abusive behavior by people in the government. Now that we live in an age of terrorism, some people are advocating that the government develop a national identity card with chips that would provide the government with data of all kinds about everyone in the country.

It is now possible, for example, to take photographs (digital, of course) of people's retinas and use these photographs in identity cards. Airline passengers who purchase these cards and pay a yearly fee can check in and get to waiting rooms for departures very quickly. This technology can also be used to see whether terrorists are trying to board planes, or to check up on who is going where, for whatever purposes the government might want to know this information.

The globalization of the world means, also, that criminal types and antisocial individuals with computer programming knowledge can use the Internet to spread destructive viruses that can disable millions of computers. Vandalism used to be local; but now, in the age of the Internet, it is global. There is now even cyber-warfare, as countries fight each other by fighting one another, so to speak, on the Internet.

New devices for recording television programs or music are continually being developed. The fastest-selling new media playing device is the DVD (digital versatile disk), and in a few years or so it is estimated that most households in the United States will have one. DVD recording devices are already on the market, but they are relatively expensive. With economies of scale, however, the price of these recording devices will fall considerably in a few years. Due to the development of the DVD, sales of videocassette recorders are plummeting; more and more people are watching films on their DVDs rather than videocassette players. The images are much sharper and the sound is better. Everywhere you look, new devices are being created and technologies that were new just a few years ago are being discarded. The world is now wired; but we do not know, at this time, what changes and effects our new technologies will have on our everyday lives and on our societies.

Despite all the new developments coming from our new technologies, as I pointed out earlier, people in America still spend an average of four hours per day watching television, and our networks and cable systems and newspapers and magazines are still controlled for the most part by media conglomerates. So the new technologies and ethnic media outlets may have some role in countering the perspectives promulgated by the media conglomerates, but they still are relatively minor voices in the scheme of things.

VIRTUAL COMMUNITIES

There is, I would suggest, something inherently alienating about the digital world that we now live in. The metaphor for digital devices is separation, a world of discrete moments and of binary oppositions—on or off, in or out, or yes or no. The digital devices we use are increasingly powerful and are able to connect us to one another in remarkable ways; but at the same time, they seem to be fostering a kind of hyper-individualism and a lack of a sense of community. We can say that global means you *can* be connected to everyone; the question is, *are* you connected to anyone? Are people less stressed in our new digital world or more stressed? Do they have less time or more time for themselves, their loved ones, and their communities?

A student of American popular culture, John Fraim, has found something very interesting about this question of the decline of community in the United States. It involves the fact that gamblers now spend more and more time with slot machines and less time with "table" gambling. He writes:

> Does the long-range movement from tables to slots mirror a similar trend in America as a whole towards less sociability? Harvard profes-

sor Robert Putnam argues American culture as a whole has moved towards less sociability in his book *Bowling Alone.* The book argues that America faces a civic crisis in that once social activities such as bowling leagues, dinner parties and community arts performances are slowly vanishing from the American landscape. Increasingly, argues Putnam, Americans are withdrawing from communal life, choosing to live and play alone. They are losing what Putnam calls "social capital" or the "glue" of trust in each other that is so essential to a democratic society.

Does the decline of table gaming and the rise in slot machine gambling suggest that more and more people want to gamble alone? Rather than being a fantasy island set off from the rest of America, Las Vegas gaming trends might offer one of the best laboratories for investigation of large scale American social trends. (unpublished manuscript, 2002)

What Fraim has discovered about changes in gambling in America suggests that our sense of community may be declining—or taking new forms, perhaps.

With the development of the Internet, new "virtual" kinds of community are evolving—for people with shared interests. There are many people who belong, if that's the correct word, to such communities and who spend many hours each day online, communicating with other members of their virtual community. Within such communities there are often dozens of interest groups in which people with mutual interests can send messages to one another. These virtual communities can be looked upon as functional alternatives to real communities, in which people know one another and there are many face-to-face interactions and shared activities.

While being a member of a virtual community does have some value, as far as helping people take care of their need for social interactions—we are, after all, social animals—I can only wonder whether the gratifications people get from being members of these communities are adequate to their needs for sociability.

Take the matter of our sexual needs. Howard Rheingold, in his book *Virtual Reality,* describes the possibilities for virtual sex in his chapter on "Teledildonics and Beyond":

The first fully functional teledildonics system will be a communication device, not a sex machine. You probably will not use erotic tele-

presence technology in order to have sexual experiences with machines. Thirty years from now, when portable telediddlers become ubiquitous, most people will use them to have sexual experiences with other *people,* at a distance, in combinations and configurations undreamed of by precybernetic voluptuaries. Through a marriage of virtual reality technology and telecommunications networks, you will be able to reach out and touch someone—or an entire population—in ways humans have never before experienced. Or so the scenario goes.

This telecommunicated sex would be made possible by people wearing close-fitting bodysuits full of sensory devices (not yet in existence) and having telesex with one another. Rheingold wrote his book in 1991, which means that this kind of sexual activity will be possible around 2021, if his timetable is correct. Woody Allen satirized the notion of mechanical devices providing sexual gratification in his film *Sleepers,* in which people had Orgasmatrons.

The question I ask is, why bother with virtual sex when real sex, between real people, is so much easier? Virtual sex, I would suggest, will probably be like virtual dining—you're still hungry after your virtual meal, or so I would imagine. Perhaps by 2021 we will have computers that eat food for us and relay sensations to our brains so we have the experience of having had a gourmet dinner without actually having had one.

Let me move on to a subject in which our participating in virtual realities of one kind or another is much more developed—video games.

VIDEO GAMES:
A BIO-PSYCHO-SOCIAL PERSPECTIVE

In 2002, the amount of money made from the sale of **video games** surpassed the amount of money made from people buying tickets to films. So we are dealing with a very important new popular culture phenomenon. There are many different genres of video games: sports games, simulations, first-person shooters, and so on. Some games can be played on computers, but most dedicated video-game players purchase game-playing consoles such as the Sony PlayStation 2, the Microsoft X-Box, or the Nintendo game cube. In the spring of 2002, Playstation 2 and the X-Box both lowered the prices of their consoles by $100 to $199 each in a price war for domination of the industry; in the summer of 2002 they lowered the prices even more.

Since video-game consoles cost around $200 and video games often cost around $50, playing video games can become quite expensive. There are other costs—biological, psychological, and social—connected with playing video games. Let me list some of them.

1. *Damage to a player's muscles* This comes from repeating the same movements over and over again with joysticks and other input devices. These repetitive stress injuries often are quite serious and need expensive medical attention.
2. *Obesity* This condition comes from a lack of exercise and from excessive snacking of fatty foods while playing games.
3. *Related medical problems* This obesity leads to other medical problems, involving heart disease (blocked arteries) and in a number of cases, juvenile diabetes. Diabetes is a serious disease; it can affect kidney functions and cause many other serious medical problems that are very expensive to deal with.
4. *Decrease in socialization with others* Some game playing is done with others, but even so, children don't have the experience

of being with lots of other children and don't develop the ability to get along with them. This can lead to a sense of alienation from others and from society, at large, especially with young people who become addicted to game playing.

5. *Hyperactivity* This kind of behavior, manifested when not playing video games, is exacerbated, perhaps, by the incredible amount of excitement generated by some of these games and the instantaneous gratifications they provide.

6. *Violence seen as a means of resolving problems* In many video games, there is an incredible amount of killing going on—as players kill aliens and monsters. Even though players know they are playing games, some of them may conclude that violence is an effective tool for doing things they want to do. There are many video games full of violence and sex, such as *Mortal Kombat V: Every Fatality, Grand Theft Auto: Vice City, BMX XXX-Acclaim,* and countless others I could name.

7. *Desensitization* In video games, players actually do the fighting and the shooting and the killing. This is different from seeing others do these things. It is possible that repeated experiences of being violent do desensitize some children, which then leads to their acting out and being violent in the real world.

You can see from this list that while individuals (and their friends) may play video games, the video-game phenomenon involves widespread medical and psychological costs, which translate to social and political costs. Private acts, we must realize, often have public consequences, and while much video-game playing is harmless, and some games provide wonderful and intellectually challenging entertainment, there are many negative aspects and social costs connected with this widespread phenomenon.

POSITIVE ASPECTS OF
VIDEO-GAME PLAYING

If there are dangers to video-game playing, there are also some benefits worth considering. James Paul Gee, a professor of education at the University of Wisconsin, argues in his book, *What Video Games Have to Teach Us about Learning and Literacy,* that video games help children learn a new kind of literacy.

These games, Gee suggests, do several things for players, such as helping them learn how to establish an identity, how to choose between different ways of solving problems, and how to get information from nonverbal cues. So there are some positive attributes to video games, and Gee suggests that they will play an important role in education in the future.

A psychologist at the University of California in Los Angeles, Patricia Marks Greenfield, was one of the first scholars to see the beneficial aspects of video-game playing. As she writes in her book, *Mind and Media: The Effects of Television, Video Games, and Computers:*

> Pac-Man and other arcade-type computer games require the player to induce the rules from observation. Computer games therefore call up inductive skills much more than did games of the pre-computer era. (1984: 111)

The visual dynamism of video games and the fact that players participate in the outcomes of these games are the primary sources of their appeal, the author argues, not the violence found in them. And, she adds, games can be developed that teach players how to cooperate rather than compete with one another.

Video games, she points out, also lead to the development of another cognitive skill, what she calls parallel processing. This skill involves players taking information from many different sources at the same time and keeping track of everything. It is this parallel processing ability that is connected, it seems likely, to the practice of multitasking, namely, doing several different things at the same time.

One danger video games pose, the author concludes, is that they are so responsive to the input of their players that they can lead to players being impatient with the rather messy way things work in the real world. But this has to be weighed against the positive attributes of video-game playing, which involve developing a sense of competence and control as well as certain motor skills involving hand and eye coordination.

The explosive development of the video-game industry in

recent years suggests that games provide numerous and powerful gratifications for video-game players. The dilemma these players face involves finding a way to navigate between the addictive and other negative aspects of video games and their positive attributes, including their potential for developing new kinds of literacy and new modes of teaching.

THE TECHNOLOGICAL IMPERATIVE

One important question we must consider when dealing with technology is whether there is some kind of a technological imperative, which means that all new technologies must be allowed to develop as much as they can, regardless of the possible consequences to individuals and to societies. We can make bombs now that can kill millions of people; should we push ahead and make bombs capable of destroying the Earth?

Many philosophers have suggested that human beings must decide how far to let new technologies develop. For instance, we might be able to clone human beings, but most people think it is a bad idea to try to do so. Some technology theorists are worrying, now, that computers and robots will soon have enough "brain power" (if that's what you want to call it) to replicate themselves and may someday dominate human beings. We will all become, according to this scenario, *servo-proteins* who exist to service the new computers and robots that will create themselves. (The fact that chess player Gary Kasparov tied an Israeli programmed computer in a match in 2003 suggests there is hope, but Kasparov is probably the best chess player alive.)

This matter of becoming *servo-proteins* is probably a far-fetched scenario, but it does pose the question very sharply: Where do we draw the line and say technological development beyond a certain point is not to be allowed? Or can we? Perhaps, as I write this, things are in the driver's seat and humankind must go along for the ride. Ralph Waldo Emerson said, in a celebrated essay (*Ode to W. H. Channing*), "Things are in the saddle, and ride mankind." I would like to think that Emerson was pessimistic and not prescient. The technological imperative theory suggests that we cannot stop technology from developing to its logical conclusion, but many philosophers have argued that not only can we limit technology for pushing beyond certain points, we must. The various *Terminator* films deal with this matter in very vivid terms.

Since it can concentrate a tremendous amount of information into the "area" of a very small text (cf. the length of a short story by Checkov and a psychology textbook) an artistic text manifests yet another feature: it transmits different information to different readers in proportion to each one's comprehension; it provides the reader with a language in which each successive portion of information may be assimilated with repeated reading. It behaves as a kind of living organism which has a feedback channel to the reader and thereby instructs him. (1977: 23)

—Yuri Lotman, *The Structure of the Artistic Text*

Ad agencies are so very useful. They express for the collective that which dreams and uncensored behavior do in individuals. They give spatial form to hidden impulse and, when analyzed, make possible bringing into reasonable order a great deal that could not otherwise be observed or discussed. Gouging away at the surface of public sales resistance, the ad men are constantly breaking through into the *Alice in Wonderland* territory behind the looking glass which is the world of subrational impulse and appetites. . . . The ad agencies and Hollywood, in their different ways, are always trying to get inside the public mind in order to impose their collective dreams on that inner stage. . . . The ad agencies flood the daytime world of conscious purpose and control with erotic imagery from the night world in order to drown, by suggestion, all sales resistance. (1967: 97)

—Marshall McLuhan, *The Mechanical Bride* ·

7

THE SOCIAL SIGNIFICANCE OF
MASS MEDIATED TEXTS

Texts—the works carried (and to some degree shaped) by the media—I would suggest are often neglected in analyses of social aspects of the media made by communication researchers. This is because, in part, media analysts and researchers are interested in making generalized statements about the media or doing statistical analyses of the media, and texts do not fit comfortably into these kinds of studies.

And yet, as I have suggested earlier, people do not watch television per se, but certain programs; and they don't just listen to the radio, but to specific stations that carry the kind of music they like or some other kind of programming to which they are attracted. The same applies to the other media—people choose to watch certain television shows, listen to certain radio stations, play certain video games, or go to particular films of interest to them. (In some cases, when people watching television are channel surfing—switching rapidly from one program to another, looking for something to amuse themselves—the composite of all the shows they have glanced at, a pastiche, can be considered a postmodern text.)

What Yuri Lotman points out, in the quotation that begins this chapter, is that texts are incredibly complex and function as rich storehouses of information for those who know how to access this material. This explains why we can read certain novels over again, with pleasure—because we get different things out of each reading. The same applies to certain films and television programs. The more you know, the more you can find in a given text. Texts may seem simple; but in reality, Lotman argues, they are incredibly complex.

Lotman has also suggested that every aspect of a text is important. As he writes, "The tendency to interpret *everything* in an artistic text as meaningful is so great that we rightfully consider nothing accidental in a work of art" (1977: 17). This means that texts are remarkably complicated, since everything in them is important, and analyzing them and interpreting them is a difficult matter. It is understandable, then, why certain great texts have fascinated readers or viewers and critics, who keep finding new things in them over the years, decades—and in some cases, such as *Hamlet* and other classics, over the centuries.

When we deal with mass mediated texts, such as films and television programs, we have to consider every aspect of these texts as important—not only the dialogue and narrative elements but also the editing and other aspects of media aesthetics, a subject that I dealt with earlier in this book.

THE TEXTS THE MEDIA CARRY
HAVE POWER

So, in thinking about the media, we must keep in mind the texts they carry and help shape. These texts have the **power,** as I have suggested in my discussion of "vicious cycles," to help shape our consciousness and give us notions about how to live, what is right and wrong, and so on. Some people get some of their social identity from television programs. For example, there are people known as "Trekkies," who attend numerous *Star Trek* conventions dressed up in *Star Trek* uniforms and buy various artifacts connected with the show. There are also groups of fans of *The X-Files* and *Star Wars*. An English program from the late sixties, *The Prisoner,* has obtained cult status.

Let me focus in this chapter upon television, since it is the medium that dominates our daily media usage. There are many different *kinds* of texts (the term used in academic discourse for these different kinds of texts is **genres**) carried by television. Some of the more important of these genres are listed in table 7.1.

Table 7.1   Genres: Kinds of Texts on Television

commercials	action adventure shows	media events
news shows	science fiction	sports shows
talk shows	religious shows	horror shows
soap operas	cooking shows	cop shows
situation comedies	music videos	plays
crime shows	documentaries	award shows

Each of these genres or kinds of programs has certain conventions that make it what it is and differentiate it from other genres. The conventions involve the kinds of characters we find, the actions they are involved in, the way they speak, and that kind of thing. As we grow up and watch different kinds of programs, we learn these conventions and become able to distinguish one genre from another. This is a kind of incidental learning that takes place; after watching several episodes of a certain genre, we learn what to expect in soap operas or cop shows or any of the other popular genres. That is, most genres are formulaic and rely, to a considerable extent, on knowledge audiences bring to the shows and desires audiences have for certain kinds of entertainment.

CONVENTION AND INVENTION IN TEXTS

A continuum exists between texts that are primarily based on convention and those that are essentially based on invention. In the mass media, because radio and television stations want to attract as large an audience as possible, texts tend to be closer to the convention side of the continuum—texts that audiences can easily understand and that don't challenge them very much. At the opposite end are the challenging works. For example, think of the difference between a television situation comedy like *Friends* and a novel like James Joyce's *Ulysses* (figure 7.1).

We can use this diagram to think about where certain films and

Convention   **Invention**

1   2   3   4   5   6   7   8   9   10

Friends   *Ulysses*

Figure 7.1   The Convention–Invention Continuum

television shows might be placed on the continuum. If *Friends* = 1 and *Ulysses* = 10, it's an interesting problem to consider where any of the following texts might fall: *Star Wars, The Matrix, Tomb Raider: The Angel of Darkness, Joe Millionaire, Gran Turismo 3, CSI, 60 Minutes, The Sims, Chicago, The X-Files, The Terminator, Alias,* and *Annie Hall.*

This continuum between convention and invention was dealt with in John Cawelti's classic study of westerns, *The Six-Gun Mystique:*

> All cultural products contain a mixture of two elements: conventions and inventions. Conventions are elements which are known to both the creator and his audience beforehand—they consist of things like favorite plots, stereotyped characters, accepted ideas, commonly known metaphors and other linguistic devices, etc. Inventions, on the other hand, are elements which are uniquely imagined by the creator such as new kinds of characters, ideas, or linguistic forms. (1971: 27)

Most mass mediated texts are conventional, but that doesn't mean they have to be. One finds a good deal of experimentation and even so-called avant garde textual practices in certain genres, such as science fiction and music videos, as well as in commercials.

THE POWER OF COMMERCIALS

In the United States, the most important television genre by far—from an economic standpoint, that is—is the commercial. It may be somewhat simplistic and reductionistic to put it this way, but as I've pointed out earlier, many critics argue that from an economic perspective, the essential thing that television does is to deliver audiences to advertisers for their commercials. The nature of these audiences is very important since different genres—and different shows within a genre—attract different kinds of audiences, with different levels of education, different degrees of sophistication, and different income levels (that is, different **demographics**).

The big hullabaloo that took place in March 2002 about David Letterman possibly moving from CBS to ABC arose because the Letterman show attracts a younger, and supposedly more affluent, audience than the show it was to replace on ABC—a distinguished and long-running news show called *Nightline.* Letterman might be paid $30 million a year, but he brings in many times that in commercials because of the audience he attracts. He decided to remain at CBS, which makes something like $170 million a year in commercials from his show.

In the final analysis, the system we have for financing television is all about attracting audiences for commercials and making money not only for the companies that advertise on television but also the stations and networks that broadcast their commercials. The price we pay in the United States for our so-called free television is advertising; commercials now take up as much as twenty minutes of a one-hour show in some cases. The average situation comedy is written to take up twenty-two minutes; the remainder of the half hour is for commercials and promos.

It has been estimated that Americans spend approximately one year of their lives just watching television commercials. Typically American teenagers are exposed to approximately 360,000 television commercials by the time they graduate from high school (some have estimated the number at closer to 500,000). So the television commercial is what makes television, as we know it here in the United States, possible. In some countries people pay fees to the government to watch television and aren't exposed to the number of commercials that we are in the United States. So our system of providing "free" television, which we pay for by allowing for commercials on our programs, isn't the only one around.

It is important to remember, also, that we eventually pay for our "free" television programs by generally being charged more when we purchase the products and services advertised on TV; the advertisers pass their costs on to consumers. We pay many hundreds of dol-

lars for advertising every time we purchase a new car. We also pay psychologically by having our attention interrupted by commercials so often.

Commercials not only affect our minds (that is, our decision making about products and services) but also have the power to affect our bodies. Due to the growth of the U.S. fast-food industry—which makes great use of commercials—an ever-increasing percentage of our children and adolescents, as well as adults, are now obese. Many suffer from clogged arteries, heart problems, and diabetes from eating all those french fries and hamburgers and other fat- and calorie-laden junk food they saw advertised on television.

In recent years prescription drug companies have started advertising, and magazines and the airwaves are full of advertisements and commercials for various prescription drugs. The people who are exposed to these advertisements then put pressure on their physicians to prescribe these drugs. This has caused incredible growth in the popularity of—and a significant rise in the price of—certain prescription drugs.

Television commercials, then, often have a social significance—in the broadest sense of the term—that goes far beyond the products they are advertising. There is a biological, psychological, and social dimension to commercials; these narratives—or perhaps micro-narratives is more correct—have important consequences.

NARRATIVES IN THE MEDIA

Our lives are saturated with media, and the media are saturated with narratives. This point is made by the French scholar Michel de Certeau, who explains in his book *The Practice of Everyday Life:*

> From morning to night, narrations constantly haunt streets and build-
> ings. They articulate our existences by teaching us what they must be.
> They "cover the event," that is to say, they *make* our legends (*legenda,*
> what is to be read and said) out of it. Captured by the radio (the voice
> is the law) as soon as he awakens, the listener walks all day long
> through the forest of narrativities from journalism, advertising, and
> television narrativities that still find time, as he is getting ready for
> bed, to slip a few final messages under the portals of sleep. Even more
> than the God told about by the theologians of earlier days, these sto-
> ries have a providential and predestining function: they organize in
> advance our work, our celebrations, and even our dreams. Social life
> multiplies the gestures and modes of behavior *(im)printed* by narrative
> models; it ceaselessly reproduces and accumulates "copies" of stories.
> Our society has become a recited society, in three senses: it is defined
> by *stories (recits,* the fables constituted by our advertising and informa-
> tional media), by *citations* of stories, and by the interminable *recitation*
> of stories. (1984: 186)

What Certeau points out is that these narratives are not simply entertainments; he calls our attention to their powerful social and cultural
significance. We learn certain physical gestures from them; we learn
how to behave in many cases by imitating those we see in these narratives, who become "models" for us. These narratives, Certeau
argues, even organize our lives and permeate our dreams.

Martin Esslin makes a similar argument. As he explains in his
book, *The Age of Television,* television is essentially a narrative
medium:

> On the most obvious level television is a dramatic medium simply
> because a large proportion of the material it transmits is in the form
> of traditional drama, consisting of fictional material mimetically rep-
> resented by actors and employing plot, dialogue, character, gesture,
> costume—the whole panoply of dramatic means of expression. . . .
> The time devoted by the average American adult male to watching
> dramatic material on television thus accounts to over 12 hours per
> week, while the average American woman sees almost 16 hours of
> drama on television each week. That means that the average Ameri-
> can adult sees the equivalent of *five to six full-length stage plays a week!*
> (1982: 7)

Esslin's figures are somewhat dated (his statistics were gathered in
1976–1977). In the last thirty years the amount of television viewing

people do each day has increased, and it is reasonable to suggest that we see more televised narratives now than in earlier times. It is the nature of these narratives, which tend to be full of violence and exploitative sexuality, and their power to affect our emotions and our ideas about ourselves and "life" that are of importance here. The term *mimesis* means "imitation," and it is to that subject, as explained by Aristotle, that we now turn.

ARISTOTLE ON NARRATIVES

We all know what narratives are—stories. But the matter is a bit more complicated. The earliest and one of the most important philosophers to write about narratives was Aristotle. In his *Poetics,* written around 330 B.C., he suggests that literary works—and now we include works such as films, television shows, novels, and plays—are always imitations of reality; that is, they can be thought of as being like mirrors. Aristotle's concept is known as the **mimetic theory of art.**

Aristotle proposes three topics that are related to imitation:

* *the medium of imitation*   language
* *the mode of imitation*   comedy or tragedy
* *the objects imitated*   men in action

He points out that some works use only language, while others use many different media. The mode of imitation involves whether a work is comic or tragic, or some combination of both. Then Aristotle moves on to the object of imitation, which he defines as "men in action." This matter of dealing with men in action he later describes as plot—namely, the structure of the interactions or arrangement of incidents in a story. So a narrative, for our purposes, is a story of men (and women) in action.

Aristotle offered rules that were observed for centuries about plots having a beginning, middle, and end (in which the action is resolved) and about the nature of comedy and tragedy, among other things. Aristotle's rules are no longer slavishly observed, but his description of the basic elements of narratives is useful for our purposes: A narrative tells a story by having characters interact with one another, and in doing so it can use many different techniques and media, involving matters such as lighting, music, sound, scenery, and costuming.

TEXTS AND OTHER TEXTS: INTERTEXTUALITY

One reason for the powerful emotional impact of narrative texts such as films and television programs is that they often draw upon (consciously or unconsciously) other texts we are familiar with—a concept known as **intertextuality.** There is a considerable amount of controversy about what intertextuality means, but for our purposes we will consider it to involve making allusion to, imitating, adapting, and modifying previously created texts, styles of expression, or genres. Often this intertextual borrowing is not done consciously by the creators of texts, I should point out, though sometimes— especially in the case of parodies—it is. Think, for example, of the *Saturday Night Live* spoofs of news programs.

In *Understanding Media Semiotics,* Marcel Danesi offers us an excellent example of intertextuality with his discussion of *Blade Runner:*

> The main text of the movie *Blade Runner* . . . unfolds as a science fiction detective story, but its subtext is, arguably, a religious one—the search for a Creator. This interpretation is bolstered by the many intertextual allusions to Biblical themes and symbols in the movie.
>
> The search for replicants in the film also ties it into postmodern thought, which is concerned with simulations of all kinds and their relation to reality. (2002: 63)

Some films pay homage, stylistically, to the works of great filmmakers such as Orson Welles and Sergei Eisenstein, other films "remake" other films (such as the lamentable remake of the Italian film *Swept Away* with Madonna), some films adapt novels, and many other examples of intertextuality can be found in all media.

The Russian literary theorist M. M. Bakhtin offers some insights

Figure 7.2   The search for a creator is one intertextual interpretation of the movie *Blade Runner.* **Can you think of examples of intertextuality in movies you've seen recently?**

into the nature of intertextuality. In his collection of essays, *The Dialogic Imagination,* he explains:

> every extra-artistic prose discourse—in any of its forms, quotidian, rhetorical, scholarly—cannot fail to be oriented toward the "already uttered," the "already known," the "common opinion" and so forth. The dialogic orientation of discourse is a phenomenon that is, of course, a property of *any* discourse. . . . Every word is directed toward

an *answer* and cannot escape the profound influence of the answering word that it anticipates. The word in living conversation is directly, blatantly, oriented toward a future answer-word: it provokes an answer, anticipates it and structures itself in the answer's direction. (1981: 279, 280)

Dialogue becomes, for Bakhtin, the basic metaphor we need in order to understand the process of communication and, in particular, the creation of texts. The basic metaphor is that of dialogue and not monologue, of conversation, not monologism (that is, talking to oneself). In our everyday conversations, for example, we rely on what has already been spoken as well as on what we anticipate might be spoken. The same applies to the arts, Bakhtin asserts.

Texts exist, then, in a kind of limbo—suspended between the past, that is, earlier texts, and the future, or forthcoming texts. All texts, it could be said, are intertextual in that they borrow from, are based on, or are affected to varying degrees by texts that have preceded them. These earlier texts have, in different ways, influenced the psyches and sense of possibility of the creators of later texts. Bakhtin's stress on the importance of dialogue (technically known as dialogism) offers us new insights into the creative process; it also shows how important the social and cultural context is for creators, of all kinds. That is because the creators of artistic texts are profoundly affected by the social and cultural milieu in which they find themselves—whether they recognize this to be the case or not. And by extension, all texts and other creative works that already exist cast a long shadow, so to speak, or provide a compelling frame of reference on all texts being created at a given moment.

In many cases artists and creative people in all media are unaware of the extent to which their work has been influenced by previously created texts; in other cases, in parody for example, artists are aware of earlier works and imitate them in a ridiculous manner. Bakhtin deals with the difficulties of separating one person's speech—by which we can read "text"—from another:

The relationship to another's word was equally complex and ambivalent in the Middle Ages. The role of the other's word was enormous at that time: there were quotations that were openly and reverently emphasized as such, or that were half-hidden, completely hidden, half-conscious, unconscious, correct, intentionally distorted, deliberately reinterpreted and so forth. The boundary lines between someone else's speech and one's own speech were flexible, ambiguous, often deliberately distorted and confused. Certain types of texts were constructed like mosaics out of the texts of others. . . . . One of the best authorities on medieval parody, Paul Lehmann, states outright that the history of medieval literature and its Latin literature in particular "is the history of the appropriation, re-working and imitation of someone else's property." (1981: 69)

So intertexuality is nothing new; the concept helps us understand why it is that some "new" texts can seem so familiar, and why texts often have remarkable emotional power. In part it is because these texts often connect—stylistically or in content—to other texts with which we are familiar.

Figure 7.3   This calculator advertisement aims to catch readers' eyes by parodying the familiar painting *American Gothic*, by Grant Wood. Do you find it effective? Did you recognize the image?

An interesting example of intertextuality is discussed in *Pulp Politics: How Political Advertising Tells the Stories of American Politics,* by Glenn W. Richardson. He discusses the 1988 presidential campaign of George H. Bush:

> The appeal of invoking associations drawn from popular culture was not lost on George H. Bush's advisors in 1988 when they considered what turned out to be one of the most important phrases the vice president would ever utter. In August, Bush's speechwriting team was sharply divided over whether to include in his acceptance speech at the Republican National Convention the now infamous line, "Read my lips: no new taxes." "Read my lips" was a catch-phrase of the hyper-macho action-film hero "Dirty Harry" Callahan, played by actor Clint Eastwood. . . . By merely aping the language of a familiar Hollywood icon, the vice president was able to activate a deep web of preexisting associations in his audience. Campaign ads can do this even more effectively, by using audio, visual, and narrative elements to tap viewers' cognitive maps, literally evoking neural networks in our brains to communicate campaign themes with emotional force. (2003: 4–5)

We see, here, how an intertextual reference to a well-known popular culture text can have enormous consequences. Much political advertising makes use of such references in their parties' print advertisements and television commercials.

THE QUESTION OF THE "UR-TEXT"

If all texts are related to one another—stylistically, based on their adoption of certain technical or genre conventions, or content-wise (that is, by imitating or alluding to a particular text)—the question arises as to whether all texts are related to one, primal, "Ur-text." This text would be a kind of template for all other texts, the "mother of all" texts. (The idea of the **Ur-text** derives from a Renaissance notion of the exemplar or archetype-book that only the angels can read. See, for example, www.artistsforum.com/koch_book2.html.)

Let me suggest that the fairy tale is the foundational model or "Ur" form of the narrative. I believe that fairy tales, which psychoanalytic critics such as Bruno Bettelheim say are the first important narratives to which we are exposed, are Ur-texts. These fairy tales, collectively, contain all the elements found in the more important contemporary narrative genres, and a given tale may contain all of them:

science fiction	characters ride on magic carpets, have magic weapons
horror	various monsters and dragons need to be dealt with
action adventure	heroes have tasks to do or battles to fight
detective	characters must solve puzzles and crimes
romance	the hero marries the princess

In modern narratives we generally find updating of these primal elements, but the origin of our more important genres can be traced back to the fairy tale and to the psychological gratifications and instructions about how one is to function in the society that these fairy tales provided.

NEWS ON TELEVISION

The 9/11 attack and the coverage of subsequent events show that television can perform a valuable service. In times of crisis, it is invaluable. At other times, however, the news falls victim to the same forces that operate on television—the need to maximize profits. At one time news was considered a service that networks provided to audiences, even if news shows lost money. Now, news—especially national news broadcasts—has been "lightened" up, and broadcast news, in general, suffers from being turned into an entertainment and increased tabloidization. Local television news is even worse and, generally speaking, can only be described as a disaster.

We can see this reflected in the story, discussed earlier, about ABC trying to lure David Letterman away from CBS (*Newsweek,* March 11, 2002). If ABC got Letterman, it would have replaced a venerable and much-honored news program—*Nightline,* with Ted Koppel, long considered one of the best interviewers and most respected journalists in television news. It turns out that *Nightline* has approximately the same number of viewers as the Letterman show, but they are older and don't attract advertisers to the degree that Letterman does.

The tyranny of audience demographics, and the quest of advertisers for younger audiences, were at work in the Letterman story. A friend of mine in the advertising industry told me recently that the hottest demographic is now ages twelve to thirty-two; advertisers are after twelve-year-olds, hoping to "brand" them and recruit them to lifelong purchasing of their products and services. Young children have also been taught to be brand conscious. I can only wonder what the impact of all this branding will be on American culture and society.

I would suggest that news and commercials are, as regards their social, economic, and political impact, the most important genres carried by television; and selected texts from these genres, I have suggested, can significantly affect our psyches, our bodies, and our society. Curiously, however, it may be the commercials we watch that have the most profound and long-lasting impact on us as individuals—especially commercials for food products that affect and in some cases shape our food preferences, and political commercials that play an important role in electing politicians and thus helping determine social policy.

THE 9/11 TRAGEDY

When it comes to the matter of the social impact of the mass media, the 9/11 tragedy is of signal importance. For people in the United States, and elsewhere as well, there are probably no television images in recent history as horrifying as those of the two planes, controlled by terrorists, crashing into the World Trade Center. These images were followed shortly by horrific images of people jumping to their deaths from the buildings, and then of the enormous buildings collapsing into a gigantic pile of rubble as smoke from the fires filled the sky. Some people who were asked about viewing these events on television said it looked like a film or television program to them.

In the primitive ritual view, sacrifice fights violence not with ordinary violence, which would simply cause the crisis to escalate, but with good violence that seems and therefore is mysteriously different from the bad violence of the crisis, because of its foundation in a unanimity that religion—that which binds men together—tends to perpetuate. If used wisely and piously, this good violence can stop the bad one from spreading whenever the latter reappears, as it necessarily must. Sacrifice is the violence that heals, unites, and reconciles, in opposition to the bad violence that corrupts, divides, disintegrates, undifferentiates. (1991: 214)

—René Girard, *A Theater of Envy:*
William Shakespeare

The most comprehensive analysis of violence on television has been conducted in the National Television Violence Study (1996) which analyzed the content of a total of 3,185 programs across 23 television channels from 6 a.m. until 11 p.m., 7 days a week, for the course of a television season. The researchers report that 57% of all programs analyzed had some violence and that one third of programs presented nine or more violent interactions. This study also examined the context within which the violence was presented and found that rarely was violence punished and rarely were victims shown as suffering any harmful consequences. . . . These patterns led researchers to conclude that not only was violence prevalent throughout the entire landscape, but that it was typically shown as sanitized and glamorized. (1998: 166)

—W. James Potter, *Media Literacy*

despite its supposedly 'entertaining' nature—alienation and gloom" (1988: xviii). Other researchers, who worked independently of Gerbner and his associates, made the following conclusions about media and violence (I have slightly modified the language of these reports for the sake of readability:

- Media exposure to violence boosts public estimates of crime and violence.
- There's a significant relationship between exposure to crime shows and approval of police brutality and bias against civil liberties.
- Television viewing was related to feelings of anxiety and fear of victimization.
- Television viewing tends to cultivate the presumption of the guilt rather than the innocence of a suspect. (1988: xviii)

It is reasonable to argue, based on the preceding statements, that television violence is not, as some theorists suggest, a harmless cathartic but has, instead, profound effects both upon individual viewers and society in general. Television may not be the direct and only cause of much of the violence that we find in American society, but it has to be considered a contributing factor. When Gerbner and Signorelli discussed terrorism, it seemed like just a minor aspect of the matter; but after the horrendous events of 9/11, terror has now become a major factor in analyses of violence. There is little question that people in the United States now feel extremely vulnerable as a result of the terrorist destruction of the World Trade Center.

A NEW LONGITUDINAL STUDY OF TELEVISION VIEWING AND VIOLENCE

A study by the Center for Media and Public Affairs shows that there has been a 17 percent drop in prime-time violence on television; broadcast violence decreased 11 percent, and violence on premium cable shows decreased 65 percent. This may represent a certain amount of progress, but a drop of 17 percent from a very high amount of violence may not be that important. We now have research indicating a strong connection—that is, correlation—between viewing television and aggressive acts.

An article by Nanette Asimov in the *San Francisco Chronicle* deals with a new longitudinal study on the relationship between television viewing and violence. It reports that young teenagers who watch more than an hour of television each day "are nearly four times as likely to commit aggressive acts in later years than those who watch less than an hour." In the article, Asimov discusses the findings of a seventeen-year study on the relation between television viewing and violence:

> The 17-year study, to be published in today's issue of the journal *Science,* studied 707 children from adolescence to early adulthood. Researchers found a "significant association" between television viewing and later violence by both boys and girls, although the effect was most striking in boys. (March 29, 2002: 2)

Jeffrey Johnson of Columbia University, a co-author of the study, suggests that parents should not let children watch more than an hour of television a day during early adolescence. His study mentions that during an average hour of prime-time television, three to five violent acts are portrayed; and an hour of children's television has twenty to twenty-five violent acts. Most of the violent acts on children's television are comic, but that doesn't mean they don't predispose children toward violent behavior.

One of the more remarkable findings deals with youths who watched three or more hours of television per day at age fourteen and acted in an aggressive manner at sixteen or twenty years of age: It turns out that 45.2 percent of males and 12.7 percent of the females acted aggressively. Of the fourteen-year-olds who watched one hour or less per day, 8.9 percent of the males and 2.3 percent of the females acted aggressively. The authors argue, also, that television viewing "remained significant" even after they dealt with other factors that may generate violent behavior, such as neighborhood violence, neglect, and psychiatric disorders.

In studies of television viewing and violence, the results are generally correlations between viewing television violence and violent

We saw the jump was between less than one hour and more than one hour a day. There was a four-fold increase. Parents should try not to let children watch more than one hour a day on the average. We are social beings and we tend to want to try out things that we see other people doing, especially if we see the person rewarded for what they did or portrayed as a hero for it. We found that teenagers who, at mean age 14, watched more than three hours a day of television were much more likely than those who watched less than one hour a day to commit subsequent acts of aggression against other people.

Source: Jeffrey Johnson, Columbia University

behavior. This is because it is very difficult to establish causal relations between anything, when dealing with human beings. But this does not mean that studies that establish correlations are of little interest. The study I have just cited, which dealt with children over a seven-year period, is the first that offers such a long-term view of the relationship between television viewing and violence. Defenders of television often argue that television may be a contributing factor in violence, but it is not the sole factor or a causal one. The important question is, to what degree is television a contributing factor?

KINDS OF VIOLENCE

There are, let me suggest, any number of different aspects of violence. To show how complicated violence can be, I have listed several sets of paired opposites that consider the various kinds of violence that exist in relation to the media.

mass mediated violence	violence we see directly
real mediated violence (wars)	fictive mediated violence (stories)
comic violence (kids' TV shows)	serious violence (adult films)
violence to individuals	violence to groups and society
police violence (just)	criminal violence (unjust)
verbal violence (insults)	physical violence (hitting someone)
violence to humans	violence to animals
"fake" violence (wrestling)	"true" violence (bar brawl)
violence against heroes	violence against villains
violence against women	violence against men
visual images of violence	prose descriptions of violence
as sign of depravity	as cry for help

Violence, as this list suggests, is an incredibly complex matter. That helps explain why our responses—both individually and collectively—to violence depend on whether we see the violence as defensive, as part of the scheme of things (in sports), as caused by hatred, as justice (by the police), or as evil (by murderers and terrorists). We feel differently about violence directed against machines or aliens than we do about violence directed against humans, and we react differently to comic violence versus serious violence. I doubt that the typical television viewer has ever articulated all these different kinds and aspects of violence, but it is quite likely that viewers can differentiate between so-called good violence and bad violence and carry in their heads ideas about the many aspects of violence just described.

One problem, for example, involves comic violence. Young children are exposed to a great deal of comic violence on many of the television programs they see. We used to assume that because it was comic it had no serious effects. Now, some researchers have suggested that exposure to comic violence has negative effects on children.

VIOLENCE IN TEXTS:
QUANTITY VERSUS QUALITY

One problem with counting the number of violent incidents in a given time period is that it neglects the specific kinds of violence and the way violence is used in a particular text. One act of violence in a particular text may have a much more powerful impact than several other acts of violence in a different text. So merely counting the acts of violence on television in a given time period may not be very useful. Because there is no universally accepted way of scaling the impact of different acts of violence in a text, however, counting the acts of violence in a given time period is the best we can do. And as the Columbia University study shows, there is a strong correlation between the amount of television viewing children and adolescents do and their tendency to be aggressive and commit violent acts, regardless of the role the violence might have played in a given text.

There is, of course, violence in many elite texts—that is, classics. Look at Shakespeare's *Hamlet,* for example. At the end of the play, the stage is littered with dead bodies. But the violence in *Hamlet* stems from the plot and is not gratuitous—unlike the violence in many contemporary films, where cars and buildings are blown up and people are killed, one after another.

In many contemporary films and television programs, there is so much violence that we have, literally speaking, "overkill." Violence loses its significance for the plots of these texts—though the impact of this violence on our psyches lingers on, I would suggest, long after we turn off our television sets or leave the movies. Many of these violence-filled films are later shown on television—which, even without these films, is permeated with violence. Consider, for example, reports of violence in news shows, comic violence in children's programs, sports violence (especially great in hockey and football), violence in cop shows and other dramatic pieces, and, of course, in televised wrestling matches—which really should be seen as theatrical performances and not a sport.

In some texts, as I suggested earlier, you may have several incidents of violence, but one particular incident may be much more important than others. In the classic western *Shane,* a pathological killer named Jack Wilson (played by Jack Palance) kills a hapless victim in a bar. But the most significant act of violence comes at the end of the film, when Shane (played by Alan Ladd) confronts Wilson in a classic shoot-out.

By the time this shoot-out occurs, the dramatic tension has built up; the violence in this scene has much more resonance and power than the other violent scenes in the film. And the audience generally feels an incredible sense of relief as Wilson finally crumples to the ground, killed by Shane—a gunslinger even faster than Wilson. So some acts of violence in a text are much more powerful and meaningful than other acts of violence in the same text. In many contemporary films, which are permeated by violence—fights, exploding cars, killings, and so on—it is often difficult to see which violent scene or event is the most significant.

VIOLENCE IN NEWS BROADCASTS

If you watch a typical local television news show, you see stories about murders, rapes, fires, automobile accidents, and that kind of thing. Local television news shows, and to some extent national news shows, are permeated with violence—in part because there is so much real violence in the world. In Oakland, California, for example, there were more than a hundred murders during 2002. So the ten o'clock news on KTVU Channel 2—the hour-long local news program from Oakland—had an incredible number of news reports about murders in Oakland, as well as reports of rapes, kidnappings, and the like that took place in Oakland and elsewhere.

Television is an audiovisual medium, and television producers are looking for stories with a strong visual element. Interviews with so-called talking heads don't have the visual power of a fire or a dead body; but they may have more importance because some talking heads have political power and their decisions can affect our lives in profound ways.

Because the violence shown in television news is "real," because television news captures events that actually happened, news violence has a status different from the "unreal" violence in dramas and narratives. This real-world violence may affect viewers differently, then, from dramatic fictions. As George Gerbner and others have suggested, it may convince viewers that the world is dangerous and generate feelings of anxiety and fear.

The question we must ask about local televised news is whether the shows could deal with other events, of more importance to community well-being, instead of the endless successions of murders, rapes, robberies, fires, automobile crashes, and other terrible things. That is, producers of local news programs select from several different possible stories to cover. They don't have to fill their newscasts with

Figure 8.1   Local television newscasts and newspapers across the country reported regularly on the 2002 disappearance and murder of a Modesto, California, woman named Laci Peterson, who was nearly eight months pregnant. Is this type of story appropriate for your local news sources to cover? Why or why not?

gossip and sensationalist stories, but they do so because they believe (and perhaps they know) that such stories attract a large audience. In other words, they claim to be giving their television viewers what they want.

This may or may not be true. The question is, should television give people what they want or seem to want (in part because they have been brought up on a diet of sensationalistic news shows) or what they need—that is, information that will make them better informed and more responsible citizens? The question regarding whether what television audiences want (or say they want) is what they've been taught to want has not been resolved and is one that still troubles media researchers.

Many critics have suggested that news programs—once regarded as a public service to the community, even though they lost money—have now become obsessed, like other kinds of television shows, with getting high ratings and making as much money as possible. Critics describe news as having undergone "tabloidization," by which they mean that news shows have too many stories about celebrities, scandals, and other events of little real importance. Occasionally, news shows feel forced to cover stories that have appeared in tabloid newspapers; such reports are full of gossip, unsubstantiated reports on celebrities, and, in some cases, political scandals. News has become, to a considerable degree, an entertainment (and many people now find it difficult to distinguish one from the other). As such, it finds itself continually relying on the crutch used by many other entertainment genres—violence.

Philip Seib offers a telling indictment of most radio and television news programs in his book *Going Live: Getting the News Right in a Real-Time Online World:*

> Real-time journalism often delivers the news in easily consumable bites. But these are intellectual snacks, not meals; they satisfy only briefly and leave a hunger for more. There is not enough substance to be truly filling. This issue is not relevant to some news reports, since the story topics themselves—especially spot news items—are shallow and inconsequential. More substantive stories—those that have long-term importance—suffer from high-speed, quick-and-dirty coverage. (2002: 58)

What people need to counter these stories, especially the ones found on local news shows that are full of murders and fires and similar material, is generally found in newspapers; they can offer context and in-depth coverage. Unfortunately, many Americans don't generally get this kind of material, since a high percentage of the American public relies on radio and television for all its news.

CHILDREN AND MEDIA VIOLENCE

A huge number of websites are devoted to media and violence— around 20,000 are listed on Google. These websites offer their readers information discovered by the numerous psychologists and sociologists and other media scholars who have made serious studies of violence in the media. The findings of the preponderance of media scholars about violence follow (taken from the websites of pediatricians, media researchers, and other interested parties):

- Media violence can lead to aggressive behavior in children. The most recent study, by Columbia University as discussed earlier, confirms this fact.
- By age eighteen the average American child will have seen 16,000 murders and viewed about 200,000 acts of violence on television.
- The level of violence during Saturday morning cartoons is higher than the level of violence during prime time. There are 3 to 5 violent acts per hour in prime time versus 20 to 25 acts per hour on Saturday morning.
- Media violence is especially damaging to young children (under age eight) because they cannot easily tell the difference between real life and fantasy. Violent images on television and in movies may seem real to young children. They can be traumatized by viewing these images.
- Media violence affects children by leading to increasing aggressiveness and antisocial behavior, by increasing their fear of becoming victims, by desensitizing them (making them less sensitive to violence and to victims of violence), and by

increasing their appetite for more violence in entertainment and in real life.

- Media violence often fails to show the consequences of violence. This is especially true of cartoons, toy commercials, and music videos. As a result, children learn that there are few if any repercussions for committing violent acts.

Many media researchers and pediatricians suggest that the amount of television children are permitted to watch be limited to one and no more than two hours a day and that parents monitor the television their children watch.

Experts also suggest that parents should not allow their children to watch violent television programs, videos, or films; and they should monitor the video games children are allowed to play. In addition, they suggest that parents must help children distinguish between fantasy and reality and explain to them that real-life violence has consequences. Unfortunately, a large percentage of parents do not monitor the television their children watch—partly because these parents use television as a baby-sitter and partly because many children (54 percent) have their own television set in their bedrooms.

Figure 8.2   Many children watch television without parental supervision or guidance.

The semanticist S. I. Hayakawa once wrote an article entitled "Who's Bringing Up Your Children?" His answer was—television.

I consulted a neurologist about mass mediated violence, and he suggested that violent scenarios may affect people by affecting their neurological system; the violent acts may become a form of conditioning. That is, they may create certain pathways and circuits to the brain and affect its neurochemistry. The brain then becomes alerted by certain acts that function as "red flags," and this can lead to physical violence or other forms of antisocial behavior.

We also know that children imitate others, so there is reason to fear that children will imitate the behavior of characters they identify with, often without realizing what the outcome of their behavior will be. They may not realize that certain behaviors have dire consequences. So there is reason to argue that young children, before the age of eight, should be shielded from mass mediated violence. We should do the same for young adolescents, and actually for everyone, since violence—even for adults—can have very negative consequences. Adults, also, as many scholars and researchers suggest, become fearful and anxiety ridden by being exposed to violence, even when they know that the violence is not real.

"KILL 'EM"

When I taught courses on media criticism, I used to ask my students to watch wrestling matches on television. It was not unusual to see some people at the match, including little old ladies, run up to the ring and scream, "kill him, kill him" to their favorite wrestler— usually a good-guy "hero" wrestler who was throwing a dirty, bad-guy wrestler around the ring, according to the script. These fans didn't want their heroes to actually kill their opponents, but their behavior shows how violence—even "fake" violence, can excite people. *There is a visceral—that is, physiological—effect from seeing violence, even fake violence,* that leads people to react in different ways. Some get very excited, some scream and cheer, some tremble, some avert their eyes.

My point is that even if we think we are old and mature enough to "handle" violence, we may be fooling ourselves; and we may be affected by it—traumatized, made anxious, made fearful, and so on. The word *violence* is very close to the word *violate,* which has all kinds of negative denotations and connotations. When we watch violent acts in the media, we are often affected in ways we may not recognize.

Since we are probably exposed to 16,000 or more murders during the course of our television viewing as we grow up, it must have some effect on us; perhaps not on most children, but those who have psychological problems and other difficulties may be more influenced by their exposure to television violence, film violence, and other mass mediated violence (in music videos and rap music, for example). These individuals are much more likely to act out and be violent, sometimes in serious ways, as they grow older.

Several solutions suggest themselves here. First, the people who make violent television shows and films and other texts must significantly reduce the amount of violence they inject into their works. There is even an aesthetic principle that makes this a reasonable course of action: The law of diminishing returns suggests that the continual use of violence dulls its impact, so producers and directors and writers serve their own interests—as well as those of society at large—by reducing the amount of violence in texts. Second, we must reduce our exposure—and especially the exposure of our children—to violent texts. During the aftermath of the 9/11 tragedy, many psychiatrists and mental health professionals suggested that it was a good idea for adults to cut down on the amount of news they were watching, since constant exposure to the horrendous images of the World Trade Center collapsing were having powerful and negative effects on viewers, both young and old.

It would also be a good idea if government or parental groups could find a way to induce the creators of television programs for children to reduce the comic violence in these shows. The airwaves, after all, are owned by the American people, and the networks and stations that use these networks are supposed to be doing so in the public interest. I recall seeing one interview with a television producer who said he won't let his children watch the shows he makes because they are too violent.

We ought surely to look in the child for the first traces of imaginative activity. The child's best-loved and most absorbing occupation is play. Perhaps we may say that every child at play behaves like an imaginative writer, in that he creates a world of his own or, more truly, he rearranges the things of this world and orders it in a new way that pleases him better. . . .

Now the writer does the same as the child at play; he creates a world of phantasy which he takes very seriously; that is, he invests it with a great deal of affect, while separating it sharply from reality. Language has preserved this relationship between children's play and poetic creation. It designates certain kinds of imaginative creation, concerned with tangible objects and capable of representation, as "plays"; the people who present them are called "players." The unreality of this poetic world of imagination, however, has very important consequences for literary technique; for many things which if they happened in real life could produce no pleasure can nevertheless give enjoyment in a play—many emotions which are essentially painful may become a source of enjoyment to the spectators and hearers of a poet's work.

—Sigmund Freud, "The Relation of the
Poet to Day-Dreaming" (1908)

9

MEDIA ARTISTS

By "media artists" I mean all the people who create texts—either individually, as in the case of most nonfiction books or a work of fiction by a novelist, or collectively, as in the case of a film or television show. In a typical film or television show, for example, we have:

performance artists	actors and actresses
production artists	directors, editors, camera operators, musicians
creative artists	writers

as well as producers, publicity people, and all those involved in the business side of filmmaking.

After the action in a film concludes, as we get up from our seats, a scroll usually appears on-screen, giving credit to many of the people who were involved in making the film. From the producer and the director and actors and actresses to the first assistant director and second assistant director down to the grips and the makeup artists, almost everyone's contribution is acknowledged.

Most films involve an incredible number of different kinds of media artists and specialists. Television programs, while usually not as complicated as films, still require the talents of many kinds of artists. For example, there are a dozen writers on the writing team that creates the situation comedy *Frasier* each week. The show that you see on television is just the tip of the creation and production iceberg, so to speak. A simple program—such as a cooking show—could easily have fifteen or twenty people involved in actually making the program.

There is a difference between writing books, which tends to be an individual effort, and making films and television shows, which is a collaborative effort. But writers of books, while they may write alone, still must take the wishes and desires of others—namely publishers and editors, and sometimes other people, such as marketing directors—into consideration. And of course, like anyone else doing creative work, writers must consider their audiences.

To show how complicated the process of creating media texts is, let me take a relatively simple kind of text—a scholarly book—as an example. For other kinds of texts, such as television programs, films, video games, and so on, you can assume that matters are even more difficult.

PUBLISHING A SCHOLARLY BOOK:
A CASE STUDY

Let's take the matter of writing a scholarly book as an example. Someone writes a book on some scholarly subject—one that may also be used in courses at colleges and universities. (I make a distinction here between *scholarly* books that are written on some subject and may be used as texts in courses and *textbooks,* which are written only for use in courses and generally have a great deal of teaching apparatus: study questions, extensive bibliographies, learning exer-

cises, and so on. In some cases, the distinction between scholarly books and textbooks is hard to make.)

Writers of scholarly books always face the problem of finding publishers who will agree to publish their books. In many cases, a writer must prepare a substantial proposal that describes the book, lists the chapters, discusses the competition, and offers a sample chapter. This is sent to editors at various publishers who publish the kind of book the author has written. Let us suppose an acquiring editor at XYZ Books likes the proposal and asks to see the book manuscript. Generally speaking, scholars send off their proposals for books before they have actually written them, so they can avoid writing a book that nobody will publish. Let us assume, now, that the scholar has written a book-length manuscript based on a proposal submitted earlier.

The acquiring editor, who is responsible for finding books to publish, must then convince an editorial committee at his or her publishing house—made up of editors, marketing directors, and others—that the book (now in manuscript form) is worthwhile. By this I mean it is a good book—well written and with sound scholarship—and it probably can find a suitable audience. It takes a considerable amount of money to publish a book, and publishers must make a profit if they are to survive. So every book published is in a sense a bet, made by the publisher, that a book will find enough of an audience to make publishing that book profitable. Publishers realize they can't win every bet; but if they don't win enough bets, and sell enough books, they go out of business.

My experience has been that editors often have many useful suggestions to make about what is dealt with in a book—about how much weight should be given to certain subjects and about what might be added to the book or deleted from it. It is not unusual for an author to get a manuscript back with long notes, questions, and suggestions on many pages of a manuscript. Once the manuscript for the book is revised to the satisfaction of the editor, he or she often sends the manuscript to some scholars and professors who are thought to be experts in the subject, to see whether there are errors of fact and interpretation in the manuscript and whether there are topics that have been missed or not explained well. So it is not unusual for an author to receive several (sometimes four or five) anonymous reviews of the manuscript, suggesting what should be done to make the book better, or, in some cases, even suggesting that the manuscript not be published.

This means there is another step that must be taken—dealing with the scholarly and professorial reviews of a book, some of which are constructive and valuable and others of which can be mean-spirited and extremely hostile. These reviews, even the negative ones, can be helpful, since they often point out areas that might need work and problems readers might face in reading the book. So the author then must take the various suggestions into consideration and revise the manuscript again, where revisions are called for.

Let us suppose now that this is done to the satisfaction of the book's editor. Next, the book is sent to a copy editor (many of whom are freelancers), who goes through the book doing things like checking for typing mistakes the author has made, smoothing the prose here and there, asking questions about facts, and checking footnotes and bibliographical citations. I have found copy editors to be extremely helpful in the course of my career. In the old days, copy editors wrote their questions on glued notes and you'd get your manuscript back with three or four notes, with questions or suggestions on them, on some pages. Now copy editors tend to ask their questions and make their changes in bold type right in the file (taken from the diskette that has the manuscript on it) and then send a printout with their questions and suggestions for the writer to consider.

The copyedited manuscript is then sent back to the writer, who answers the copy editor's questions, makes sure the meaning of the text hasn't been changed, and approves of any changes the copy editor has made.

When the manuscript has been copyedited and then examined by the author, it is then sent to a production editor, who is responsible for the design of the book and its eventual production. Production editors then send the manuscript to book designers, who decide on the typography of the book—what typefaces are to be used, what size the text block should be, how much spacing there should be between lines of type, and where illustrations are to go and how large or small they should be. The production editor generally tells the designer how many pages the book should be, and the designer works within those guidelines. The production editor also must arrange to have a cover designed for the book. Sometimes the typography and cover design are done by artists who work for the publisher; at other times, the typography and cover design are sent out to freelance book designers and cover artists.

When the typographer has done with the manuscript, it is sent to the printers, who set the book into type following the instructions of the book designer or typographer (often using computer files the author has sent). The printers run off page proofs and send them to the author, who must check over the page proofs for errors made by the typographer and for errors in the book that the copy editor and author missed. The author then must make an index or have the page proofs sent to a professional indexer. Once the index is made, the page proofs can be sent to the printer and the book manufactured.

You can see, then, that while it took only one person to write the book, it takes numerous people to move the book manuscript into production and actually publish the book. Although this process is less complicated with novels, editors often play an important role with novel writers—getting them to cut or expand their manuscripts and make various changes here and there—so novelists also generally work with their editors. One reason editors are important is that writers become so involved with their manuscripts that, in a sense, they can't see them clearly. Someone who is not so emotionally tied to a book can often see things that need to be done to it to make it better.

Writing scholarly books and novels is a lonely occupation. You sit in front of a computer (it used to be a typewriter) and spend hours putting words down, one after another. But once you have a manuscript that has been accepted by a publisher, you find yourself dealing with many book publishing professionals, with different areas of expertise, who work with you in turning your manuscript into a book.

THE BOOK BUSINESS

It's interesting to compare the audiences for books and other mass media, such as television programs. We can make a distinction between trade books, which are produced for the general public and sold in bookstores; and scholarly books, which are written for scholars but often used in university courses; and textbooks, which are produced for students and generally not sold in bookstores. Publishers sell scholarly books and textbooks by printing up catalogues describing their books and sending them to professors who may find the book of personal interest and may also want to use it in some course they are teaching. Most publishers now have sites on the Internet, where their books are described and where people can arrange to purchase them. Trade books generally have only a three-month "window of opportunity." If they don't sell well during that period, they are typically remaindered, or sold to companies that grind them up and reuse the paper pulp.

A trade book that sells 100,000 copies is considered a great success, while a network television show that attracts only 6 or 8 million viewers (and thus has poor ratings) is often considered a failure. Some trade books, of course, sell in the millions; but the average book is lucky if it sells five or ten thousand copies, and the average scholarly book doesn't sell anywhere near that number of copies. Textbooks are a different matter. A good textbook, in a core subject (such as an introduction to economics or a reader for freshman English), can sell tens of thousands or even hundreds of thousands or millions of copies.

New technology has now come to the aid of the writers and publishers of scholarly books. The minimum press run that makes economic sense for a scholarly book is between 500 and 1,000 copies, though in many cases the press runs are much larger. But some scholarly books don't sell anywhere near a thousand copies, which means the publishers—usually university presses—have stacks and stacks of previously published scholarly books in warehouses, which costs them money. Now, due to the development of new print-on-demand printers, which can print a cover and the text of a book from a CD-ROM in just a short period of time, scholarly book publishers can print their books on demand. That is, they can print books when they get orders for them—and avoid large inventories of books, many of great scholarly importance, that may or may not find purchasers. And inventories of previously published books can be disposed of, without the book going out of print.

Several commercial print-on-demand publishers, such as IUniverse and Xlibris, enable authors to "publish" a book for as little as $150 or $200. For this money authors get their book set into type (from a computer file the author must provide) with a cover designed for the book. When anyone orders one or more copies, they are printed "on demand," so to speak.

What this means is that anyone with a computer and $150 or $200 (and up, for fancier versions of a book) can now publish a book with companies such as Xlibris and IUniverse. These books are available to the general public and are described and listed at sites such as Amazon.com and BN.com (Barnes & Noble). It isn't a way to make a lot of money, but people who write books that may not be commercially viable can still publish them at very low cost. Before print-on-demand machines were developed, authors who couldn't find a regular publisher for their books had to use vanity publishers (in reality, printers who specialized in publishing books for authors who couldn't find regular publishers), and it generally cost thousands of dollars to have one's book manufactured.

SCRIPT WRITING AND
ABERRANT DECODING

Let us move from books to television. Technically speaking—using communication jargon—we can say that writers of scripts for televised programs, such as sitcoms, dramas, or documentaries, "encode" a communication, assuming or hoping that their audiences will "decode" their communication correctly—that is, they will "get" what the writer wanted them to get and will interpret the text the way the writer wants them to interpret it. These terms—*encoding* and *decoding*—come from linguist Roman Jakobson's model of communication: A sender encodes a message and sends it, using some medium, to a receiver who decodes it. This model also applies to films as well as all kinds of other mediated texts.

We sometimes find, in our everyday lives, that in our conversations we say something to someone who, for one reason or another, doesn't interpret what we said correctly. This misinterpretation could

be for any number of reasons, such as our receiver didn't know some of the words we were using, couldn't hear everything we said, didn't notice the tone we used in saying what we said, wasn't paying attention and missed some of what we said.

When it comes to the mass media, and the sender is the writer of a film or television show, or a member of a team of writers, for example, the opportunities for "receivers" (that is, audiences) misinterpreting what's in a text grows exponentially. This misinterpretation is known as **aberrant decoding.** Umberto Eco, a semiotician who has written extensively on popular culture, has suggested that aberrant decoding tends to be the rule when it comes to the mass media. That is, people generally don't decode texts the way the media artists who create them expect them to be decoded. He writes:

> Codes and subcodes are applied to the message [text] in the light of a general framework of cultural references, which constitutes the receiver's patrimony of knowledge: his ideological, ethical, religious standpoints, his psychological attitudes, his tastes, his value systems, etc. (1972: 115)

This problem becomes widespread with the development of the mass media, since there is often a considerable difference in the **class** and educational levels between the writers of mass mediated texts and the audiences for these texts. For example, writers may mention famous artists and philosophers or works of art that most members of their audience may never have heard of, or writers may allude to important events that the audience members do not know about.

This means that writers for the mass media have to be very careful not to write material that's "over the heads" of their audiences. They must keep their target audience in mind, though this doesn't mean that everything on television has to be "dumbed down" so it can appeal to, and be understood by, the so-called lowest common denominator of the viewing public. In some cases, the target audience is a relatively small (in percentage) number of people who watch elite programming on public television channels or on regular television networks or cable. These particular target audiences may not be large, but the people in these audiences tend to be affluent opinion-makers whose influence is considerable and whose purchasing power is of interest to select advertisers.

MEDIA ETHICS AND JOURNALISTS

Ethics is that branch of philosophy having to do with what might be described as "right conduct." Many different philosophical arguments have been made about what is and what isn't ethical behavior, what ethics should deal with, and related matters. When we come to the media, several different areas involving ethics suggest themselves.

Consider journalists, for example. Journalists are supposed to work under a code of ethics that requires them to report the news honestly and accurately—by which we generally mean avoiding putting their own interpretation or "spin" on what they cover. Some critics have suggested that all news involves interpretation, even when reporters wish to be accurate. Reporters also should avoid even the appearance of any conflicts of interest. For example, a journalist who writes about the stock market for a newspaper should not write an article praising a company in which he or she has invested.

One problem journalists sometimes face is in reporting about events that cast a negative view on advertisers who spend a great deal of money in the newspaper or television station that employs the journalist. This problem is often faced by editors, who must decide whether to run a big story that they know one of their important advertisers doesn't want them to run. Some editors deal with negative stories about such advertisers by burying them in a back section of the newspaper or by mentioning them only briefly on television news shows.

Journalists often face ethical dilemmas. Those who get information from people about some case being tried in the courts have often refused to give this information to prosecutors or even reveal who gave them the information. Many journalists have spent time in jail for refusing to hand this kind of information over. That is because they have given their word to their informants that they wouldn't tell who gave them the information or hand it over. The notes a journalist has taken, for example, are considered private and privileged. The same applies to footage shot by television journalists in interviewing people for news programs.

Ideological and financial matters also generate ethical problems for journalists. The news editors at newspapers and radio and television stations have to decide what stories to run—from all the stories they could run. Is a story about a murder-suicide more important than a story about a speech by a senator or congressperson? And how should that speech be characterized? What should be emphasized and what neglected? In many cases, ideological matters may be even more important than financial ones. Political partisanship colors what stories are run and the perspective the reporter takes. Newspapers and radio and television stations are generally owned nowadays by giant corporations, which have political agendas.

ETHICS AND ADVERTISING 1: SELLING CANCER

Other ethical problems are faced by media artists of all sorts. For example, think of the dilemma copywriters and art directors face in advertising agencies that have tobacco accounts. These artists and copywriters are asked to use their talents to sell a product that medical evidence has proven leads to cancer. It may be legal to purchase cigarettes; but for copywriters it is not moral, I would suggest, to use one's literary and artistic skills to convince people to purchase cigarettes or any tobacco product.

In other cases, copywriters are asked to sell products that don't work (such as diet remedies), aren't good for people (certain foods), or are dangerous (sport utility vehicles). On the other hand, people who work in advertising agencies often have families to support, and they may feel that they cannot put their job or their family's welfare at risk. Advertising executives often argue that they are only providing people with information, and it is up to each individual to decide what to do with that information. Others say, "If we don't do tobacco ads, some other agency will, so we'll do these ads even if we really don't want to do them." Of course, some agencies refuse to handle these kinds of accounts—especially tobacco accounts—which, I would argue, is the moral thing to do.

ETHICS AND ADVERTISING 2: PORTRAYAL OF WOMEN

Advertising agencies (and the companies that employ them) have frequently been attacked for the way they portray women in print advertisements and commercials. The overwhelming number of female models we see in the glossy advertisements in magazines and newspaper pages are unusual physical specimens, looking as if they are anorexic or nearly so. The images of these models give women the notion that they must be slender if they are to be glamorous and beautiful. These models also perpetuate the notion that women should define themselves as "sex objects" to be gazed at and lusted after by men, and not as active, forceful individuals. Women are also frequently portrayed in narrative texts as victims who are saved by male heroes.

As Anthony J. Cortese writes in *Provocateur: Images of Women and Minorities in Advertising:*

> Attraction is both socially constructed and biologically shaped to
> be an instantaneous decision. Whether a female is attracted to a male
> or vice versa is based on unconscious biological signals of sexual inter-
> est. Just as female animals are attracted to power and exhibitions of

strength in males of the same species as signs of health and fertility, human females are drawn toward displays of masculine power and strength. . . . For females, a small waist . . . and a high-pitched voice are signs of vulnerability that appeal to a male's self-identification, through cultural transmission, as a protector.

Large pupils are sexually appealing and this dilation occurs unconsciously during arousal. . . . Youth is also a sign of health and sex appeal. . . . Women use foundation makeup to hide small wrinkles, because eliminating any signs of aging contributes toward a more desirable and attractive image. Skin tones are warmed up in order to project a healthy sexual glow.

An exaggerated leg length appears to be more adult and, therefore, more sexual. . . . Hair grooming is also an important component of attraction and gender display. . . . A smile symbolizes approval or attraction. . . . Unconscious blushing is considered to be very sexual. . . . How female breasts are displayed is a key part of sexual attraction. The cleavage area between the breasts is perhaps the epicenter and stimulation of interest. In fact, breast cleavage and the cleavage of the buttocks are considered to be very sexual. In truth, there is a great similarity between the appearances of the two types of cleavage. (1999: 21, 22)

Cortese points out that our notions of what makes a woman beautiful are culturally and socially determined, though he reminds us that sexual attraction also has a biological component.

At different times through history, our notions of what makes a woman beautiful have changed. At one time we liked curvaceous and full-bodied women; but in recent years we have favored very slim, almost boyish-looking women. Attitudes about what makes a woman beautiful are also connected to socioeconomic class, ethnicity, and a number of other variables. We look at the average advertisement for only two seconds; but those two seconds are enough, some theorists suggest, to register in our psyches and affect our behavior.

This exploitation of the female body has been attacked by feminist critics, social scientists, and others as having negative effects on both men and women. Men and women both are given unreal images of what an ideal woman is like—young, long-legged, glamorous, wasp-waisted, satin-skinned, and inflamed with sexual desire that is generally shown by their body language, display of cleavage,

Figure 9.1   The woman in the skin care advertisement (top) has normal-sized pupils. In the makeup ad (bottom) the model's pupils are partially dilated. Large pupils are often used in advertising to suggest sexual appeal.

and facial expression. In recent years, advertisers find that they can use extreme close-ups and show only parts of women to create the sexual tension and excitement they seek to generate, a device known technically as *synecdoche* (a part stands for the whole, or vice versa).

ETHICS IN ADVERTISING 3:
POLITICAL COMMERCIALS

For the last fifty years, the practice of running "attack ads" in political campaigns has grown considerably. In these highly negative commercials and print advertisements, candidates are attacked for something they supposedly did or something they said or some policy they supported or some vote they cast. That is, the ad doesn't say what a politician believes, but attacks his or her opponent. In many cases, the makers of these attack ads play loose with facts and the truth, for political advantage. The general public always says, when polled, that they hate these ads—but attack ads, especially commercials, have been shown to be very effective.

As Montague Kern writes in *30-Second Politics: Political Advertising in the Eighties:*

> By 1986 negative advertising, which focuses on the opponent rather than a candidate in terms of both issues and character, was . . . considered to be a necessary evil by representatives of all the schools [of media consultants]. (1989: 208)

And negative advertising in "attack commercials" is with us today more than ever.

The danger in using these negative attack ads is that politicians who use them are thought to be mean-spirited and nasty; the danger in not responding to such ads with negative attack ads of one's own is that candidates allow these attack ads to portray themselves to voters in ways that they can't live down. Politicians who use attack ads often find surrogates to do the attacking, and the same applies to politicians who respond to attack ads with their own counterattack ads.

Those who are attacked in these negative political ads have learned to go on the offensive immediately, before the attack ad can

Figure 9.2   Even though we can't see the whole woman, her leg is shown to represent the whole person. This is an example of synecdoche.

take hold of people's imagination. The counterattack ads often assail the credibility and truthfulness of the politician behind the attack ad. What this means is that political campaigns have become very negative in recent years, with politicians and parties attacking and counterattacking one another.

Some political scientists have suggested that one reason politicians use attack ads is that they want to get average voters (who generally vote for Democrats) so fed up with the process of voting that they don't vote. This means that conservative politicians generally will do better because a high percentage of their constituents tend to vote.

One of the most famous negative attack commercials was the "Revolving Door" ad during the 1988 presidential campaign. It suggested that Dukakis, the Democratic candidate, was "soft" on crime, and was titled "The Dukakis prison furlough program." (The commercial was made by the Frankenberry, Laughlin & Constable ad agency.) The commercial opens by showing prison guards walking along a barbed-wire fence, and then there's a close-up shot of prisoners going through a revolving door. A caption superimposed on the screen reads: "268 escaped." Next comes a medium shot of the prisoners going through the revolving door. The following caption reads: "And many are still at large." Then there's a dissolve to a wide shot of the prison wall, the guard, and the guard tower.

An announcer, in a voice-over, reads the dialogue attacking Dukakis as the images of the prisoners in the revolving door and the guards remain on the screen:

> As Governor, Michael Dukakis vetoed mandatory sentences for drug dealers. He vetoed the death penalty. His "revolving door" prison policy gave weekend furloughs to first-degree murderers not eligible for parole. While out, many committed other crimes, like kidnapping, rape. And many are still at large. Now Michael Dukakis says he wants to do for America what he's done for Massachusetts. America can't afford that risk.

Dukakis didn't respond immediately to this commercial, and as a result, found himself on the defensive during the rest of his campaign. He had allowed the Bush campaign to define Dukakis as "soft on crime" with very gripping and, it turned out, long-lasting images that stuck in people's minds.

The people who make these attack ads—the political consultants, the copywriters, the art directors, and all the others involved in these activities—must realize that their behavior can be construed as highly questionable, from an ethical point of view. Perhaps they justify it by thinking, "all's fair in love and war—including political campaigns as part of war."

Perhaps they think it is so important to get their candidate elected that other matters, like whether the attack is fair, are considered unimportant. But that seems very close to arguing that the ends justify the means, a philosophical position that says "anything goes" and is counter to the American belief that the means are tied to any ends and using "evil" means for "good" ends corrupts these good ends.

Jeffrey Scheuer makes an important point about political adver-

An Erratic GOP TV Commercial

One of the most notorious television commercials of the year 2000 presidential campaign was run by Republicans and referred to a drug prescription plan offered by the Democrats. In the commercial, there is one still shot, on the screen just briefly, that displays the word *RATS*.

Figure 9.3

Some media critics have suggested the Republicans did this to use **subliminal** suggestion and to connect, in the minds of viewers exposed to these commercials, Democrats and rats. The people who made this commercial denied that this was their intent. A neurologist I asked about subliminal suggestion said he thought it had been proven to be effective.

tising in his book, *The Sound Bite Society: Television and the American Mind*:

> It is a truism of our media-dominated age that television has largely usurped the traditional role of political parties. Power flows to those who control (or can afford to buy access to) the airwaves. The gate-keepers are the arbiters of visibility, such as Ted Koppel and Larry

King, and their corporate media-masters; party bosses have been
replaced by pollsters, media advisers, and direct-mail consultants. Vir-
tually all political actions and communications—not just political ads
but also floor speeches by legislators, news conferences, debates, and
party conventions—are designed expressly for consumption as sound
bites by a TV audience. (1999: 29)

In his book, Scheuer describes the degree to which conservative
political forces dominate television and other media.

Media artists, we see, have tremendous power; their words, their
images, the narratives they create, the songs they write have audiences that often number in the millions. The same, of course, applies
to those who perform the works that media artists create. With this
power comes a great responsibility—one that too many writers and
artists (and all the others connected with creating and performing
texts in the various media) do not, so it seems, want to accept.

In the dictionary the mass is defined as the great body of the people of a nation, as contrasted to some special body like a particular social class. Lazarsfeld and Kendall use such a definition when they write "The term 'mass' then, is truly applicable to the medium of radio, for it more than the other media, reaches all groups of the population uniformly." This notion of the mass merely implies that a mass communication may be distinguished from other kinds of communication by the fact that it is addressed to a large cross-section of a population rather than only one or a few individuals or a special part of the population. It also makes the implicit assumption of some technical means of transmitting the communication in order that the communication may reach at the same time all the people forming the cross-section of the population.

—Eliot Friedson, "Communication Research
and the Concept of the Mass,"
American Sociological Review

There is no "mass" communication because there is no "mass" audience. Instead, there are many audiences, some with structures and leadership and others without these characteristics. Some audiences last only a few hours (Super-bowl viewers) while others last for a whole season (diehard football fans). Some audiences are based on a need for immediate information (viewers of CNN), some on in-depth information (readers of news magazines), some on a need for a religious experience (viewers of the PTL Club), some on a need for political stimulation, musical entertainment, romantic fantasy, and on and on. . . . Each of us is a member of multiple audiences. You are a member of a local community that the local newspaper and cable TV franchise targets. You are a member of virtual communities when you are on the Internet—communities that quickly form and may last for only one evening. You are a member of certain hobby groups that are targeted by certain magazines. (1998: 246–247)

—W. James Potter, *Media Literacy*

10

THE MASS CULTURE/
MASS SOCIETY HYPOTHESIS

I n this chapter I deal with an argument that was very popular a number of years ago—that the mass media were turning America into what was known as a "mass society." I will call this "the mass culture/mass society **hypothesis.**" The theory was that **mass culture** inevitably led to a mass society, in which individualism was destroyed and a slave-like "mass man" (and now we'd say "mass woman") was created. Although this debate about mass culture stems from the 1950s, it is still relevant today—and perhaps, due to the increased power of the media, it is even more important now than it was when it was originally propounded.

THE MASS CULTURE HYPOTHESIS:
MYTH OR REALITY?

In America there is, I would suggest, a kind of diffuse obsequiousness toward European philosophers, culture critics, and theorists of one sort or another. Culturally speaking, we Americans still see ourselves, I would argue, as spiritual orphans, as "sons and daughters" who have abandoned our intellectual motherlands and fatherlands in Europe and elsewhere, in a desperate but futile attempt to escape from history or, more precisely, an historical consciousness (though, of course, we probably have half the historians in the world in America).

Our intellectuals and deep thinkers on cultural matters, espe-

I'm a cretinized
dehumanized
alienated
mass-man.

cially those found in literature departments and communications departments, now bend their knees to French cultural theorists more than those from other countries. (Fifty years ago it was German thinkers who dominated our theorizing, as I shall explain shortly.) We derive many of our concepts and ideas, as far as cultural criticism is concerned, from the likes of Roland Barthes, Claude Lévi-Strauss, Jean Baudrillard, Jacques Derrida, Jean-François Lyotard, and one could go on and on here—with occasional Russians, Bulgarians, Italians, Germans, and others bringing up the rear, so to speak.

ROUND UP THE INDICTMENTS, OR, THE LANGUAGE OF CRITICISM IN THE FIFTIES

In recent years the critics of American media and culture don't seem to be as certain about things as they were in earlier times. Perhaps the demise of Communism and the questions many now raise about Marxism have contributed to this feeling. In the fifties, however, many American intellectuals and others interested in media, culture, and society learned and became indoctrinated, one might say, into the jargon of some social theorists and culture critics who had fled from Germany and other countries in Europe. Let me cite two examples from German scholars:

In an important collection of essays, *Mass Culture: The Popular Arts in America* (published in 1957), Gunther Anders explained to us, in his essay "The Phantom World of TV," that "Modern mass consumption is a sum of solo performances: each consumer, an unpaid homeworker employed in the production of the mass man." This leads, he adds, to the creation of mass-produced hermits who don't want to renounce the world but, instead, want "to be sure they won't miss the slightest crumb of the world as image on a screen." Eventually, he predicted—tongue-in-cheek, perhaps—we would lose our ability to talk. "Because the receiving sets speak in our place, they gradually deprive us of the power of speech, thus transforming us into passive dependents."

T. W. Adorno is represented in the book with an essay, "Television and the Patterns of Mass Culture," that suggests "popular culture is no longer confined to certain forms such as novels or dance music, but has seized all media of artistic expression." The media, for Adorno, seem all-powerful. He describes modern mass culture as repetitive, boring, and ubiquitous and suggests that these aspects of modern mass culture "tend to make for automated reactions and weaken the force of individual resistance." Eventually, he adds, people not only lose their ability to see reality as it is, but their capacity for life experience may be dulled.

WHERE ARE THE MASS MEN AND MASS WOMEN THE CRITICS OF THE FIFTIES WARNED US ABOUT?

The theorists we have been discussing believed that popular culture and the mass media would automatically generate mass culture. It, in turn, would lead to the development of mass man and mass woman—the cretinized, dehumanized, moronized, kitsch-loving, de-individuated inhabitants of mass societies that—as an additional and ominous feature—lent themselves to becoming totalitarian. This would happen because, and this is implicit in the arguments of the early elitists, the media would affect everyone in more or less the same way. According to these theorists, individuals living in mass societies were essentially isolated or atomized and thus were highly susceptible to messages from the media.

This theory, that the media not so much affect or shape but actually determine the consciousness of individuals, is very close to what used to be called the "hypodermic" theory or "magic bullet" theory of the media, a theory that is now generally discredited and considered simplistic. According to this theory, discussed earlier, messages in the media are interpreted in essentially the same way by everyone, and these messages generate responses that are direct and more or less automatic and immediate.

We now recognize that things are not as simple as the hypodermic theorists thought they were and that such matters as race, religion, age, ethnicity, **gender,** education, values, personality, and a host of other variables affect our decisions about the media we will watch or listen to and the way we respond to the texts carried by this media. This does not mean that the media don't have effects on large numbers of people, but there is good reason to argue that the effects are not universal and not everyone is affected the same way.

There is some question in my mind as to whether mass culture actually exists or can exist. Of course there are countries, such as America, where an enormous amount of media are available to people; but is that the same thing as mass culture? The Eastern European societies, under the thumb of Russia and national Communist parties, were subjected to forty years of totalitarian rule and continual propaganda and a rigidly controlled mass media, but the people in these countries ditched the Communists with hardly a second thought when they discovered that the Red Army wouldn't be invading them.

DOES POPULAR CULTURE
DESTROY OUR ABILITY
TO ENJOY ELITE CULTURE?

According to Adorno and some other theorists of mass culture, popular culture "drives out" elite culture; and as people become more and more exposed to popular culture, they lose their interest in the elite arts as well as their capacity to enjoy them. This may sound plausible in theory, but in practice it doesn't seem to work out very well.

Let me offer a case study here that most people have some experience with and put the theory to the test. Take fast foods, and, in particular, McDonald's hamburgers—one of the most important symbols of American culture. As the theory goes, because McDonald's is fast and relatively cheap, the chain will drive out other kinds of restaurants that are less technologically advanced and involve individual choice (delicatessens, coffee shops, regular restaurants, ethnic restaurants, and so on). Then, following the logic of the elitist theorists, eventually we will have only McDonald's and other fast-food restaurants in America and, ultimately, all over the world because we have lost our taste for "good food."

I think we can see, from our own experiences, that fast-food restaurants have not driven other restaurants out of business. (These fast-food restaurants do have a social cost, however, which I've alluded to earlier. As a result of their popularity, childhood and adult obesity are now growing at an alarming rate, along with many ailments tied to obesity such as diabetes and heart disease.)

People use fast-food restaurants for their own purposes, and do not necessarily lose their capacity to enjoy other kinds of foods. Just the opposite happens frequently. In the San Francisco area where I live, for example, there has been an explosion of Thai and Vietnamese restaurants; and as other ethnic groups settle in America, other ethnic foods become increasingly popular. The same applies to upscale French and Italian restaurants.

I wrote an essay forty years ago, "The Evangelical Hamburger," in which (perhaps somewhat tongue-in-cheek) I suggested that the dynamics of the McDonald's hamburger restaurants was similar to

evangelical Protestantism and that McDonald's would spread all over the world. Many people thought that idea simply ridiculous. I also suggested, playing with the Marxist concept of "embourgeoisement" (which argued that capitalism was generating bourgeois, middle-class mentalities) that McDonald's involved "hambourgeoisement" and functioned so as to convince people that they were middle class because they had ready access to ground meat. We now see this evangelical thrust in the incredible growth of the Starbucks coffee shops. The argument that popular culture will destroy the so-called elite arts—and, in this case, French, Italian, and other ethnic restaurants— doesn't appear to have come true.

ARE WE BECOMING HOMOGENIZED?
ARE THE MASS MEDIA UNIFORM?

One assumption of mass culture theorists is that the mass media are, in some way, uniform and thus can perform their task of destroying our sense of individuality and making Americans, and people in other countries, mass men and women. But a look at the media shows that there is a great deal of competition in a given medium, such as television or magazines, and among the media, for the attention of people. The growth of video games, for example, has been explosive. (There has, of course, been a great deal of consolidation of control of the media—a subject I deal with in another chapter.) The networks are continually battling one another for viewers, since they must deliver audiences to advertisers to make money. Most of what the networks carry is highly formulaic junk, of course, but even formulaic genres can be done well from time to time.

In the world of magazines, we find incredible diversity. There are magazines for every interest conceivable, and some that are not conceivable. In addition to regularly published magazines, there are also huge numbers of "zines," small specialty publications on everything from ecology to Zen that are put out by individuals or groups. Now that computers and laser printers are inexpensive, it is easy and cheap for people to publish their own zines or makes their views known on their own websites. Many individuals now have become publishers, with their creations on a website on the Internet. Blogging (keeping online journals) has become an important part of the Internet now, also.

So there is good reason to question the assumption that the media are **culturally homogenizing** us and can perform the needed "mobilization" of people required to create a mass society. Rather than finding a mass society in America (and the same would apply

Figure 10.1   There are magazines for every interest, including business, sports, cooking, fashion, travel, arts, politics, and entertainment.

to many other countries) we find just the opposite—what might be described as cultural and pop cultural pluralism, with large numbers of subcultures and groups putting out their own publications, making their own films, broadcasting their own radio and television shows. This does not mean, however, that these groups all see themselves as estranged from American culture.

MASS CULTURE AND THE MELTING POT

With this discussion of popular culture, the mass media, and the theory of mass society as a background, we can now gain some insights into the question of whether there have been fundamental changes in American society and culture in the last few decades, and if so, what role the media might have played in this matter.

If the mass media were as powerful as elitists believed they were, how do we explain the fact that American society has so many subcultures and groups based on everything from race, religion, and ethnicity to political persuasion and geographic location? We are not diminished by having these various social entities, but enriched.

Urban geography is helpful in gaining an understanding of what America was like thirty or forty years ago. When we look at cities then (and today, as well) we find that they are often divided up into enclaves, in which we find the population is predominantly Italian or Jewish or black or Irish or Chinese or some other group. In the old days, these groups often had publications written in their "old-country" languages and directed toward their particular interests. It would seem that the fabled "melting pot" was more a theory of what some analysts think happened or would like to have happened than a description of what America was like fifty or seventy-five years ago. Or even today, in many cases.

Lots of different ethnic groups were thrown, so to speak, into the pot (American society). But they didn't melt into one smooth homogenous mass; they maintained their identities, even while they went about finding their place in America and realizing or trying to realize the American Dream.

Proponents of the mass society thesis would have to argue that though America may not be monolithic now, it once was because of the exposure of immigrants and others to our ubiquitous and all-powerful mass media. If the media are as powerful as they are supposed to be, how did the earlier American resist becoming unified into a mass society? And why haven't we remained a mass society?

It could be argued, perhaps, that the mass media no longer are as effective as they once were in unifying Americans and giving them a common frame of reference, with some kind of a consensus and national consciousness. But Americans are exposed to more media than they were earlier. We watch enormous amounts of television, the most powerful medium, and have VCRs to capture other shows, so we can do time-shifting. DVDs are now wildly popular, and devices such as TiVo enable us to time-shift with great ease. The growth of cable and satellite television means that huge numbers of channels are available to viewers and new technologies are being developed that will open as many as five hundred channels to viewers in the near future. (What all the channels of communication will

Figure 10.2   How much control do the mass media have over us?

carry is another matter—essentially the same old genres found in the movies and on television, with an occasional mixture of genres, such as MTV, or single-genre stations, such as all-news stations.)

The existence of a society full of subcultures and characterized by what I've described as popular cultural pluralism (some might say anarchy) suggests the media are not as all-powerful as we, or, more precisely, some communications theorists, once thought they were. It also suggests that our notion of America as a huge melting pot was more an illusion (by consensus of historians and social scientists) than a reality. Though various groups in the melting pot didn't melt, they were still in the same pot.

CHANGE AND CONTINUITY IN AMERICAN CULTURE

Societies are always evolving, so it would be incorrect to argue that there have not been changes in America. The question is whether these changes mark radical new directions in which our society is moving, or whether they are more evolutionary. America, it is often said, is a country continually undergoing revolution; thus change is the constant and not the different arrangements we make in the way we live. This notion, that we are continually undergoing change, differs from a conservative perspective that argues, as I see it, that there have been no fundamental changes in American culture and society or that the changes have been minimal.

My argument would be that in America, everything is always in the process of change and evolution. The question is, what is the nature of the changes and how do these changes relate to continuities in American society and culture?

MASS CULTURE AND AMERICAN SOCIETY: THE MYTH OF THE MONOLITH

In an essay in the September–October 1992 issue of the magazine *Public Perspective,* "The Polarization of America: The Decline of Mass

Culture," Paul Jerome Croce argues that mass culture has lost its ability to shape consensus. Croce suggests that this decline is a fundamental cause of what he sees as an increasingly polarized America:

> Through their popularity, the mass culture's productions shaped taste, established goals and values, and defined the kind of people most people thought they should be.

This consensus has now broken down, he adds, and we now find ourselves in a post-mass-culture society in which mass culture has "metastasized, with individuals still pursuing distant styles, but doing so in clusters broken off from a single massive standard."

I don't believe we ever had the "single massive standard" Croce thinks we had, or that the mass media ever had the power he suggests it had to shape a society. And I don't think we ever were as "unified" as Croce thinks. Mass media tends to reinforce values we already have—such as individualism, equality, freedom, and achievement. The media tend to reflect the societies in which they are found; although, of course, they also affect them. There's always been a great deal of conflict in American society, between classes, among races, between geographic sections of the country, and to some degree among religious groups.

People who burn with "passionate intensity" and belong to subcultures, groups that attack this or that aspect of our society, are nothing new. We have a long history of utopian communities and morally defined groups such as the Abolitionists. (We still have 40,000 people living in communes, it turns out.)

What the mass media do, I would suggest, is reflect the changes going on in society at a given point in time. They may add impetus to them and speed things up, they may be involved in **agenda setting,** they may increase our awareness and show us things many of us don't like, but I find it hard to believe that they ever had the ability to homogenize us the way they allegedly did. We never were unified to the extent Croce believes, except, perhaps, in terms of our basic values, so the media are being attacked for not doing what they did not and could not do. There are plenty of other reasons to find fault with our mass media, but we can dismiss this charge against them— that they no longer unify our society—as incorrect.

America, if the postmodernist theorists are correct, is a society in which elite art and popular culture no longer are seen as distinct and in which eclecticism and fragmentation are the norms. And this has been the case since around 1960 when the postmodernist mind-set took over. What all this suggests is that American society is one in which diversity is celebrated, in which differences are accepted—as part of the scheme of things. Rather than splitting apart, everything is getting mixed up, yet different groups still are able to maintain their identities. That, in fact, is the story of America—a country of immigrants, where people from many different nations come in search of the American Dream. Different groups may have different versions of this dream and take different paths to realize this dream, and may be different in many ways—but there still is a commonality behind these differences.

As evidence of this, let me mention a recent poll that was taken of Hispanics in America. The survey (conducted by New California Media between November 2001 and March 2002) discovered that Hispanics want to assimilate into America, that they believe there's too much immigration in America, that they think residents of America should learn to speak English, and that they are, in fact, not as unified as we used to believe they were. "A large majority of Hispanics born in the United States speaks English better than Spanish," as a matter of fact, and there's a high degree of English literacy among foreign-born immigrants who prefer to speak Spanish. The Latino National Political Survey, in a report titled "Latino Voices," concludes that "the results should dispel any notions that their political attitudes separate them from the majority of the American population or define them as a monolithic interest group."

What this survey suggests is that the United States is truly a multicultural society in which various subcultures exist. However, multiculturalism doesn't mean separateness and alienation but, rather, a different kind of coexistence. Our mass media and popular culture have neither turned us into a mass society (on the road to totalitarianism) nor made us one in which "the center cannot hold."

The tensions and anxieties found in America have been generated, in large measure, and exacerbated by the unfair and grossly distorted distribution of income that has occurred here, especially since

1980, with the poorest segments of our society actually losing ground and large numbers of people in the middle classes not gaining any ground. It is politics, not popular culture, that is most responsible for our social disorganization; and it is political decisions that will lead to the amelioration of the situation in which we find ourselves, not our popular culture or mass media.

Only 11 companies now control most of the daily newspaper circulation. In magazine publishing, a majority of the industry's total annual revenues now goes to two firms. Five firms control more than half of all book sales. Five media conglomerates share 95% of the recording market, with Warner and CBS between them controlling 65% of that market. Eight Hollywood studios account for 89% of U.S. feature film rentals. Three television networks earned over two thirds of the total U.S. television revenues. . . . These figures within an industry *underestimate* the degree of concentration, because the powerful companies own properties in more than one media industry. For example, a newspaper corporation might own several radio and television stations and perhaps a magazine or two. (1998: 225)

—W. James Potter, *Media Literacy*

What I am calling the Electronic Right comprises a broad alliance of elected officials, journalists, broadcasters and intellectuals, whose access to the media is supported by deep conservative reservoirs such as the Sarah Scaife and Carthage foundations (both controlled by Richard Mellon Scaife) and Olin, Smith-Richardson, J.M., and Bradley foundations. This policy-marketing machine sponsors an assortment of leading think tanks (such as the Heritage Foundation, American Enterprise Institute, Cato Institute, Hudson Institute, Manhattan Institute, and the Hoover Institution); various newspapers, magazines, journals and media pressure groups; conferences and seminars, books and articles, research studies, speaking engagements, editorial briefing sessions, and Internet projects; "astroturf" (fake grassroot) campaigns; radio and TV shows, including the public television programs of William F. Buckley, Peggy Noonan, William Bennett, and Ben Wattenberg among others; and sundry antitax and antiregulatory organizations. Foundations on the left have vastly inferior resources. (1999: 42–43)

—Jeffrey Scheuer, *The Sound Bite Society: Television and the American Mind*

11

MEDIA IN SOCIETY

I have just examined the "mass society" thesis of certain social critics, who suggest that the mass media are leading to a society in
which there is no sense of community and mass culture will lead,
inevitably, to a breakdown of democracy. This critique is, I suggested, a highly suspect one—and not based on convincing evidence.
In this chapter I will deal in a more general way with the media in
society—with topics such as media consolidation (and its possible
consequences), the cultural imperialism hypothesis, the problem of
pornography, and government regulation.

MEDIA CONSOLIDATION

Robert McChesney has argued, in his essay "The Global Media
Giants" (available on the Internet at www.fair.org/extra/
9711.gmg.html), that there has been a continual and accelerated
process of concentration in the media in the United States and glob-
ally as well. He writes:

> The global media system is now dominated by a first tier of nine giant
> firms. The five largest are Time Warner (1997 sales: $24 billion), Dis-
> ney ($22 billion), Bertelsmann ($15 billion), Viacom ($13 billion),
> and Rupert Murdoch's News Corporation ($11 billion). Besides
> needing global scope to compete, the rules of thumb for global media

giants are twofold: First, get bigger so you dominate markets and your competition can't buy you out. Firms like Disney and Time Warner have almost tripled in size this decade. Second, have interests in numerous media industries, such as film production, book publishing, music, TV channels and networks, retail stores, amusement parks, magazines, newspapers and the like. The profit whole for the global media giant can be vastly greater than the sum of the media parts. A film, for example, should also generate a soundtrack, a book, and merchandise, and possibly spin-off TV shows, CD-ROMs, video games and amusement park rides. Firms that do not have conglomerated media holdings simply cannot compete in this market.

These five media giants control an enormous amount of the media produced and spread throughout the world by the corporations they control. And they have numerous advantages over companies that cannot match their global reach.

There are, McChesney adds, four other "first tier" media conglomerates—enormous, in their own right, but not comparable to the first five media giants. Among these are Sony (its 1997 sales were $48 billion), which owns Columbia & TriStar Pictures and major recording interests; and Seagram (its 1997 sales were $14 billion), which owns Universal Studios and various music interests. And there are a number of second-tier media conglomerates, as well. These two tiers of transnational global media conglomerates control most of the media in the world.

Ben Bagdikian, former dean of the School of Journalism at the University of California in Berkeley, was one of the first scholars to call our attention to this matter. As he explains:

> In 1982, when I completed research for my book [*The Media Monopoly*], 50 corporations controlled half or more of the media business. By December 1986, when I finished a revision for a second edition, the 50 had shrunk to 29. The last time I counted, it was down to 26. [When an edition of *The Media Monopoly* was published in 1993, the number was down to 20.] A number of serious Wall Street media analysts are predicting that by the 1990s, a half-dozen giant firms will control most of our media.
>
> Of the 1,700 daily papers, 98 percent are local monopolies and fewer than 15 corporations control most of the country's daily circu-

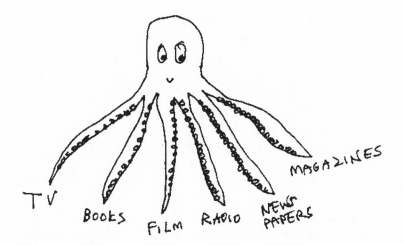

lation. A handful of firms have most of the magazine business, with Time, Inc. alone accounting for about 40 percent of that industry's revenues. (available on the Internet at www.fair.org/extra/best-of-extra/corporate-ownership.html)

The **consolidation** of media companies that Bagdikian and McChesney talk about has taken place in other areas connected to the media. There are, for example, just four or five giant global advertising corporations that own most of the important advertising agencies. Companies that want to hire advertising agencies now demand, in many cases, that they be part of these global conglomerates so the advertisers can have a global reach.

The question that arises now is—what difference does it make? McChesney offers an answer:

> On balance the system has minimal interest in journalism or public affairs except for that which serves the business and upper-middle classes, and it privileges just a few lucrative genres that it can do quite well—like sports, light entertainment and action movies—over other fare. Even at its best the entire system is saturated by a hyper-commercialism, a veritable commercial carpet bombing of every aspect of human life. As the CEO of Westinghouse put it (*Advertising Age*, 2/3/97), "We are here to serve advertisers. That is our raison d'etre." (available on the Internet at www.fair.org/extra/9711.gmg.html)

He mentions that the fifty corporations that control the media have connections with many other media organizations, which helps the media giants consolidate their power. The media giants also have political desires and interests that affect their programming and the editorial stances they take in their publications.

It may be that the giant media organizations counter one another on certain political issues and that they do serve the **public** in certain areas—fighting racism and promoting safe sex to counter the AIDS epidemic, for example. It is also possible that their size makes it possible for these organizations to take chances with artists and filmmakers that others cannot afford to do. For example, poetry books do not sell well, and if all publishers put out only books that had a good chance of making a profit, very few poetry books would be published. But publishing poetry books by serious poets can be looked upon as a public relations gesture by these companies, more than anything else.

ON CULTURAL IMPERIALISM: THE COCA-COLONIZATION HYPOTHESIS

The **cultural imperialism** thesis holds that the United States and a few other First World countries that export their films and television programs and other popular culture to the rest of the world are also

---

Quality Newscasts

"Television stations owned by big, out-of-town companies tend to produce lower-quality newscasts than those owned by smaller groups, a study by a journalism think tank has concluded. Newscasts at stations owned by large television networks fared poorly in the study. It was released Sunday by the Project for Excellence in Journalism, affiliated with the Columbia University School of Journalism. . . . The five-year study, which examined roughly one-quarter of the nation's local TV stations, gave an 'A' grade to only 11 percent of the stations owned by the 10 biggest media companies. Thirty-one percent of stations owned by small groups earned the top grade."

Source: Associated Press, Monday, 17 February 2003.

exporting their capitalist ideologies and value systems with this material. It isn't that America is consciously trying to indoctrinate people in the Third World; what happens is that writers and filmmakers and television producers quite naturally make works that reflect their values—values they have learned while growing up in America. But these values, such as the belief in the self-made man and woman and the importance of consumption, then are spread all over the globe.

Most Third World countries can't afford to make films and television programs. It is much cheaper to import works from First World countries; and with these works those countries are also getting, without recognizing it, First World ideologies and values. Thus, American and other First World cultures are not only dominating more fragile Third World cultures but also destroying them. The spread of our films and television shows and our McDonald's hamburger restaurants and Starbucks coffee shops is, according to this theory, leading to a kind of worldwide **cultural homogenization.** Eventually, according to the logic of this argument, every place will look like every other place—people everywhere will drink Coca-Cola or Pepsi, eat at the same fast-food joints, dress the same, and watch the same films and television shows.

The **cultural imperialism** theory assumes that the media are extremely powerful; if they aren't, then the effects of our media will not be significant. American media will be essentially a source of entertainment and not a force for Americanizing and changing the fundamental value systems of these cultures.

Herta Herzog dealt with this question in some research she conducted on how people in Germany "decoded" or made sense of the widely popular (at the time) television series *Dallas*. As she explained, in an important article titled "Decoding *Dallas*":

> Critics of popular culture, and of things American in particular, have concerned themselves with the question of whether the worldwide diffusion of programs such as "Dallas" made possible by the growth of the new media technologies may eventually result in worldwide cultural assimilation at the expense of indigenous diversity. (*Society*, 1986: 74)

Herzog's study of the way *Dallas* was interpreted in Germany led her to write, "The answer to my initial question—do viewers in different

Figure 11.1 Movie-goers in Kuala Lumpur, Malaysia, wait in line next to a poster of *Spider-Man*. In an unusual move, the superhero's film opened in this Southeast Asian country a few days *before* it started showing in the United States.

countries read popular culture differently?—must be answered affirmatively" (1986: 77).

Of course, she was dealing with the way one First World country, Germany, interpreted a text from another First World country, the United States. But her finding, that people in different cultures interpret texts in different ways, is a compelling reason to suggest that the media imperialism theory may be a bit overblown and that the impact of our media and popular culture on other cultures may be somewhat superficial. In recent years many countries have been scheduling American television shows in late hours, replacing them with their own shows that are more closely tied to the culture involved. But American movies still are dominant everywhere.

A NOTE ON IDEOLOGY
AND THE MEDIA

What's really important, critics of the media argue, is the way these media giants can dominate political discourse and gain their ends—to make further expansion and consolidation possible—and shut out competition. As the folk saying goes, "He who pays the piper, calls the tune." The owners of the media are the ones who call the "tunes," nowadays—they publish their tunes in the newspapers, magazines, and through book publishers they own; they broadcast their tunes on their radio stations and television stations and cable networks; they make CDs of their tunes; they make video games of their tunes; and since we hear only their tunes, for the most part, their tunes are the ones that stick in our minds and that we find ourselves humming.

By *tunes* I mean something much broader than songs—namely political viewpoints, ideological positions, attitudes, notions, and ideas. **Ideology** is generally defined as a system of logically coherent beliefs about the social and political order. The giant media conglomerates can help shape our ideologies in many different ways. First, their newspapers and radio and television stations function as **gatekeepers** and determine what stories they want to cover and which ones they will exclude or give scant attention. Second, the *way* the news media organizations cover stories affects the opinions of readers and viewers and listeners of news programs. As I mentioned earlier, what we see on television is always something that someone has determined we will see (and other things we won't see).

THE PROBLEM OF PORNOGRAPHY

Beauty, as they say, is in the eye of the beholder; and so, it seems, is determining what is and what is not **pornography.** Where does one draw the line between the increasingly revealing sexual advertisements and commercials that flood our magazines and airwaves and cable media and so-called soft-core pornography, and then between soft-core pornography and hard-core pornography?

There is also the question of whether pornography is harmful to children or others who are exposed to it—and who, as is often the case, go seeking it. The Internet is full of pornographic sites; and older children and preteens, who are curious about sexual matters, often go searching for these pornographic sites. One of the problems

---

Fighting Media Conglomerates

Many organizations attempt to fight the power of the media conglomerates. What follows is a call for papers by an organization, the Union for Democratic Communications, for a conference on "Democratic Communications and Global Justice." A list of the subjects they wish to have discussed will give you an idea of their interests:

> The Union for Democratic Communications invites the submission of paper and panel proposals, media projects, and workshops addressing the role of democratic communications in the struggle for global justice. We seek submissions with a critical* take on existing media structures and practices, such as the continuing global concentration of the media, the commercialization of new media technologies, the creeping influence of advertising from the classroom to the newsroom, the distortion and suppression of news and information by the mainstream media.
>
> We also seek submissions that highlight struggles for global justice from the local to the global level; from preserving communities and cultures to protesting meetings of the world's rich and powerful. The Union for Democratic Communications is a group of communications researchers, theorists, educators, journalists, media producers, policy analysts, and activists. The UDC is dedicated to the critical study of communications establishments and policies; the production and distribution of democratically controlled media; the fostering of alternative, oppositional, independent, and experimental production; and the development of democratic communications systems at local, regional, national and international levels.

*The term *critical* here means the UDC is concerned with offering an ideological critique of the media and the government agencies and media conglomerates that control the media.

---

involved in dealing with pornography, then, is that it is difficult to find a definition that everyone can agree upon. Pornography is, like many concepts, hard to pin down.

In a governmental paper, "US Media in the 1990s: III: The Media and Society" (available on the Internet at http://usinfo. state.gov/usa/infousa/media/media1cd.htm), Frederic A. Emmert writes:

Although the courts have long held that media publishing or broadcasting obscenity and pornography do not enjoy First Amendment protection, it remains hard for a judge to define those terms. Consequently, in the 1973 "Miller versus California" and "Paris Adult Theater versus Slaton" cases, the U.S. Supreme Court rejected the notion of a national obscenity standard and left the definition and regulation of obscenity up to "contemporary community standards defined by the applicable state law."

The Supreme Court concluded, then, that there was no way to define obscenity in a manner that everyone could accept, and left the matter of defining it up to local communities. Obviously, cultural matters come into play, and in large, international cities such as New York and San Francisco, people may have a much different notion of what is "obscene" than those in more conservative rural communities.

Emmert did explain how the Supreme Court believed communities could determine whether some text was obscene or not. He summarizes the Court's findings as follows:

The Court, however, proclaimed a general test for obscenity to be:
1) whether the "average person, applying contemporary community standards" would find that the work, taken as a whole, appeals to the prurient [sexually exciting] interest.
2) whether the work depicts or describes, in a patently offensive way, sexual conduct specifically defined by the applicable state law, and
3) whether the work, taken as a whole, lacks serious literary, artistic, political or scientific value.

As you can see, there are a great many loopholes here—which probably explains why the Supreme Court decided to let cities and states fight the matter out. For one thing, a text "taken as a whole" has to be prurient; and it also, as a whole, must lack "serious literary, artistic, political or scientific value." That means parts of texts may be "prurient" but if the whole text isn't, or if the text is a serious work of art, the work cannot be considered pornographic. In addition, a text must depict or describe sexual conduct "in a patently offensive way" that is defined as illegal by state laws.

A SUPREME COURT DECISION ON
"VIRTUAL" CHILD PORNOGRAPHY

On April 16, 2002, the U.S. Supreme Court rendered a verdict involving virtual child pornography and struck down a bill, the Child Pornography Prevention Act of 1996, as infringing on first amendment rights of artists and writers. This bill made it criminal to create "virtual child pornography, distribute it or possess it." The Supreme Court, by a vote of 6 to 3, argued that the bill was an infringement on the rights of free expression guaranteed by the First Amendment of the Constitution. The First Amendment reads "Congress shall make no law . . . abridging the freedom of speech."

Justice Kennedy, who wrote the opinion for the majority, explained that the prohibition in the Child Pornography Prevention Act of 1996 involved "any visual depiction" and was not concerned about how an image was produced:

> The section [in the law] captures a range of depictions, sometimes called "virtual child pornography," which include computer-generated images, as well as images produced by more traditional means. For instance, the literal terms of the statute embrace a Renaissance painting depicting a scene from classical mythology, a "picture" that "appears to be of a minor engaging in sexually explicit conduct." The statute also prohibits Hollywood movies, filmed without any child actors, if a jury believes an actor "appears to be" a minor engaging in "actual or simulated . . . sexual intercourse." (available on the Internet at www.supremecourtus.gov)

Justice Kennedy's point, then, which he develops at length in his statement, is that the law could be used to prevent people from having access to great works of art or even lesser works that might have sexual content that some people find objectionable. He also wrote that "the government has shown no more than a remote connection between speech that might encourage thoughts or impulses and any resulting child abuse."

We can see, then, that deciding what is obscene and pornographic is not an easy thing to do, and that attempts by the government to "protect" children may, unwittingly, dampen free expression and have very negative consequences.

One problem legal experts face in dealing with artistic texts is that texts are complicated and difficult to analyze and find consensus on—by critics, moralists or anyone. As I pointed out earlier, all kinds of aesthetic factors are involved in such texts, so it is hard for anyone to "prove" that a work is obscene, especially since in postmodern societies the barriers between everything seems to have been obliterated. We must remember that James Joyce's *Ulysses,* one of the greatest novels of the twentieth century, was once held to be obscene and was allowed into the United States only after a lawsuit brought by Bennett Cerf of Random House.

In 2002 a museum in New York City had an exhibit on contemporary art. In the exhibit was a "work of art" called *Cloaca,* which I heard about on a report on National Public Radio. *Cloaca* is, its creator says, a work of art—a machine that is fed food, grinds it up, and then, after it passes through various tubes, "defecates" what it has been fed. I believe it was created in the Netherlands, where its "excrement" was packaged in plastic and sold to people—until it was found that the excrement could not be protected from bacteria and started putrefying. Some people consider *Cloaca* to be a cosmic joke, and others think it is a wonderful work of art. In an art world in which almost anything goes, who is to say what is serious art and what isn't? And who is to say what is pornography and what isn't?

SPIRAL OF SILENCE: PUBLIC OPINION AND POLITICAL IDEOLOGY

There is a theory of communication that helps us understand how certain ideas can become dominant in society. It was developed by a German scholar, Elizabeth Noelle-Neumann, who wrote, in an important article in the *Journal of Communication* ("The Spiral of Silence: A Theory of Public Opinion") that people who believe—whether correctly or not—that they represent the majority opinion have a tendency to make their views known, while those who believe they represent the minority opinion have a tendency to keep quiet. This is because people don't wish to be isolated, and those who hold what they think is a minority view often convince themselves that their view is wrong. As Noelle-Neumann explains:

> He may find himself on one of two sides. He may discover that he agrees with the prevailing (or winning) view, which boosts his self-confidence and enables him to express himself with an untroubled mind and without any danger of isolation, in conversation, but cutting those who hold different views. Or he may find that the views he holds are losing ground: the more this appears to be so, the more uncertain he will become of himself, and the less he will be inclined to express his opinion. (1974: 44)

When some people speak up and others remain silent, there starts "a spiraling process which increasingly establishes one opinion as the prevailing one" (1974: 44). This is exacerbated because people often underestimate the number of people who share their views and overestimate the number of people who oppose them.

It is quite obvious that the media play an important role in shaping public opinion, since what people read in the newspapers, hear on the radio, and see on television news programs (where many people in America get most of their news) has an effect on what people believe is the prevailing opinion on many different issues. Noelle-Neumann's theory suggests, then, that the media help shape public opinion rather than just reflecting it.

There is some question about how effective the media are in shaping public opinion. Although a small number of giant corporations control the media, there are some countervailing forces that often play an important role in shaping public opinion. We find, for example, that many groups with important issues—based on race, ethnicity, gender, and religion—are increasingly making their voices heard, with beliefs that often are critical of the agendas and practices of the giant corporations and media conglomerates. These groups are often able to use and exploit the press for their own purposes. In addition, the political parties have an important role in affecting public opinion, especially regarding political and ideological issues.

And events often play an important role in shaping public opinion. For example, the collapse and bankruptcy of the Enron Corporation, at one time the seventh largest corporation in the United States, exposed the degree to which it and other energy producers had helped shape the government's energy policy. It also showed how a giant accounting firm, Arthur Anderson, wasn't monitoring Enron and giving honest reports about its financial status. In February 2003, a congressional committee discovered that Enron had also found a way, in collusion with banks and other financial institutions, to avoid paying its fair share of taxes. This has led to many politicians saying we have to change the tax system so corporations cannot find ways to avoid paying taxes. So shaping public opinion isn't quite as simple as it might seem, and the **spiral of silence** might not always function the way Noelle-Neumann thought it would.

GOVERNMENT REGULATION AND DEREGULATION OF BROADCASTING

Congress established an agency in 1934, the Federal Communications Commission (FCC), to regulate the broadcasting industry subject to the "public interest, convenience and necessity." The purpose of the agency was to promote diversity in broadcasting and so it issued, over the years, a number of different rules about how many radio and television stations a corporation could own in one city and rules about newspapers owning television stations in a city.

With the growth of cable, which does not use the public airwaves, the FCC has started relaxing its rules on the ownership of radio and television stations by newspapers in a city, about consolidation of ownership of radio and television stations, and about the ownership of cable television systems by television networks and media organizations. The FCC also decided to stop enforcing the "Fairness Doctrine," which mandated that broadcasters provide equal time for different points of view on issues of importance. Some members of Congress tried to reinstate the Fairness Doctrine but have been unable to do so.

In his book, *The Sound Bite Society: Television and the American Mind,* Jeffrey Scheuer discusses recent developments in the broadcast industry relevant to the matter of deregulation:

The modest balancing mechanism of the Fairness Doctrine was rescinded in 1987; and the public interest standard, as a basis for relicensing stations, has become a national joke; the fox rules the chicken coop. Mark S. Fowler, the first FCC chairman under Reagan who theorized that television is just "a toaster with pictures," deregulated with a vengeance, even lifting rules prohibiting program-length commercials aimed at children. (1999: 43)

He goes on to discuss the giveaway to the broadcasting industry of the new digital frequency spectrum, a resource also owned by the public, valued at $70 billion. This outraged some conservatives like Bob Dole, who called it "the biggest single gift of public property to an industry in this century":

I should add that under the George W. Bush administration, deregulation is moving ahead very rapidly and it looks like the broadcasting industry and the media conglomerates will get just about everything that they want in the way of relaxed rules and regulations from the FCC. There are ideological implications to this relaxation of control over the media conglomerates, which we can see, for example, when it comes to television. (1999: 45)

Scheuer discusses the so-called liberal bias to the press and points out that in reality, the networks and public television have a conservative bias. He writes:

For all their alleged liberal bias, in recent decades, the networks and public television have been decidedly more hospitable to the showcasing of centrist and conservative voices. With rare exceptions, guests on public affairs programs are fonts of conventional wisdom, typically powerful Beltway insiders with views running the gamut from right to center. The fulcrum of debate on the talk shows is even further to the right: for every centrist or moderate liberal on the left side of the screen (e.g., Shields, Germond, Carlson, Clift, Caraville, Stephanopolous), there is a crown on the right and center-right: Barnes, Bay Buchanan, Pat Buchanan, Buckley, Gergen, Glassman, Kondracke, Krauthammer, Kristol, Limbaugh, McLaughlin, Matalin, Novak, Safire, Snow, Stassinopolous, Sununu, Wattenberg, Will, et al. (1999: 47)

Scheuer points out, also, that the mainstream media tend to interview people from conservative and centrist think tanks more than from those on the left, and that newspaper opinion pages tend to be conservative, as well. He cites an interesting statistic in this respect: Richard Nixon in the 1968 election and George W. Bush in the 2000 election received somewhere between 60 percent and 80 percent of the endorsements in daily newspapers. We can see, then, that media conglomeration has social and political implications and is not just an economic matter. But we must remember that despite all the endorsements he received, George W. Bush received fewer votes than his opponent, Al Gore.

There is an attempt being made in 2003 to establish liberal talk shows on radio to counter the domination of the radio waves by conservative (and in some cases right-wing) talk-show hosts. We have to realize that radio talk shows are political entertainments, and the people working on the proposed liberal talk shows claim that they will offer talk-show hosts as entertaining as their conservative counterparts. They also hope to have their talk-show hosts on radio stations that have large numbers of liberal talk-show hosts, rather than wedging them in, as was done in the past, between conservative talk shows.

ETHNIC MEDIA:
A COMPLICATING FACTOR

As America becomes ever more multicultural, with large numbers of people from Asia, Africa, Europe, and South and Central America moving here, we find that the power of ethnic media is growing. The notion that America is a so-called melting pot in which ethnic groups quickly lose their ethnic identities and become Americanized, as I suggested earlier, doesn't seem to be working. At least in the short run. A better **metaphor** for the United States would be something like a beef stew, in which each component (that is, each ethnic group) retains its identity, while being part of something bigger than itself.

What has happened is that people from various ethnic groups

move into areas where other people from their ethnic groups live, establishing what a *Wall Street Journal* article on the growth of ethnic media called "islands of ethnic communities." The article "Ethnic Media Muy Popular in California," by Pui-Wing Tam (23 April 2002), reports on a survey of ethnic media use in California:

> Ethnic media are pervasive: Fully 84% of the survey's Hispanic, Asian-American and African-American respondents say they get information through ethnic television, radio and publications. Ethnic-media consumers are loyal: 68% of respondents say they prefer ethnic TV stations of English channels for watching news.

These various ethnic media outlets provide different perspectives from the major U.S. media outlets. But General Electric is buying Telemundo, a major Hispanic network, and other media conglomerates either own or will probably purchase other ethnic media organizations, lest these conglomerates not be able to reach increasingly large ethnic sectors of American society.

Figure 11.2   In addition to major metropolitan areas, cities all across the United States have rapidly growing ethnic populations. Oscar Erives, shown here, publishes *Buenos Días Nebraska,* the biweekly Spanish-language newspaper in Grand Island, Nebraska.

The relation between the media and society, we see, is a very complicated matter; and it is not easy to make generalizations about this relationship. There is, as I've pointed out, considerable evidence of increasing consolidation of control of the media by giant corporations, but for the long run it isn't easy to assess what impact this consolidation has had (and will have) on our culture, our political order, and our society.

GLOSSARY

aberrant decoding   When audiences decode, make sense of, or interpret texts in ways that differ from the ways the creators of these texts expect them to be decoded, we have aberrant decoding. Aberrant decoding is the rule, rather than the exception, when it comes to the mass media, according to the semiotician Umberto Eco.

administrative research   Administrative research deals with ways of making communication by organizations and other entities more efficient and more effective. It makes use of statistics and other empirical means of collecting data. Administrative research contrasts with critical research, which has more of an interest in social and economic justice, politics, and related considerations.

agenda setting   This theory argues that the institutions of mass communication don't determine what we think, but do determine what it is that we think about. In so doing, they set an agenda for our decision making and thus influence, in important ways, our social and political life.

artist   For our purposes an artist is not only someone who does paintings or sculptures or plays musical instruments, but anyone involved in the creation or performance of any kind of text—especially mass mediated texts.

attitudes   Social psychologists use the term *attitude* to refer to a relatively enduring state of mind in a person about some phenomenon or aspect of experience. Attitudes usually are either positive or negative, have direction, and involve thoughts, feelings, and behaviors (tied to these attitudes).

audience   When we deal with audiences of the mass media, we mean people who watch a television program, listen to a radio program, attend a film or some kind of artistic performance (symphony, rock band, etc.). The members of an audience may be together in one room or in many different places. In the case of television, we often have families in which each member of the

203

family watches different programs from his or her own set. In technical terms, audiences are addressees who receive mediated texts sent by some addresser.

broadcasting   We use the term *broadcasting* to deal with texts that are made available over wide areas by using radio or television signals. Broadcasting differs from other forms of distributing texts such as cable casting, which uses cables, and satellite transmission, which requires "dishes" to capture signals sent by the satellites.

class   A class, from a linguistic standpoint, is any group of things that has something in common. We use the term *class* to refer to social classes, or, more literally, socioeconomic classes—groups of people who differ in their income and lifestyle. Marxist theorists argue that there is a ruling class that shapes the ideas of the proletariat, the working classes.

codes   By *codes* we mean systems of symbols, letters, words, sounds—or whatever—that generate meaning. Language is a code. It uses combinations of letters that we call words to mean certain things. The relation between the word and the thing the word stands for is arbitrary, based on convention. In some cases, the term *code* is used to describe hidden meanings and disguised communications.

cognitive dissonance   *Dissonance* refers to sounds that clash with one another, are unpleasant, and cause pain and anxiety in listeners. According to social scientists, people wish to avoid ideas that challenge the ones they hold—ideas that create conflict and other disagreeable feelings. *Cognitive dissonance* refers, then, to ideas that conflict with ones people hold and generate psychological anxiety and displeasure. People seek to avoid cognitive dissonance.

collective representations   The great French sociologist, Emile Durkheim, used this concept in explaining that people are both individuals, pursuing their own aims, and social animals, who are guided by the groups and societies in which they find themselves and whose ideas come from these groups. Collective representations are, broadly speaking, texts that reflect the beliefs and ideals of groups and other collectivities.

communication   For our purposes, *communication* is a process that involves the transmission of messages from senders to receivers. We often make a distinction between communication using language—that is, verbal communication—and communication using facial expressions, body language, and other means, or nonverbal communication.

communications   Communications, the plural of the term *communication,* refers to messages, to what is communicated, in contrast to the process of communication, just described.

concept   We will understand *concept* to be a general idea or notion that explains or helps us understand some phenomenon or phenomena. For example, Freud uses the concepts *id, ego,* and *superego* in his psychoanalytic theory to explain the way the human psyche operates.

consolidation   *Consolidation* refers to the phenomenon in which most of the media companies are now controlled by ever smaller numbers of corporations.

critical research   Critical approaches to media are essentially ideological; they focus on the social, economic, and political dimensions of the mass media and the way they are used by organizations and others, allegedly to maintain the status quo rather than enhance equality. This concept contrasts with administrative research.

cultivation theory   *Cultivation theory* argues that television dominates the symbolic environment of its audiences and gives people false views of reality. That is, television "cultivates" or reinforces certain beliefs in its viewers, such as the notion that society is permeated by violence and we live in a dangerous world.

cultural homogenization   *Cultural homogenization* is used to suggest that the media of mass communication are destroying Third World cultures and regional cultures in specific countries, leading to a cultural sameness, standardization, or "homogenization."

cultural imperialism   Supporters of this theory, which is sometimes known as "Coca-colonization," argue that the flow of media products (such as films and television programs) and popular culture from the United States and a few other capitalist countries in Western Europe to the Third World is colonizing people in these countries. Along with these texts and popular culture, it is alleged that values and beliefs (and, most importantly, bourgeois capitalist ideology) are also being transmitted, leading to the domination of people in Third World countries.

culture   From an anthropological perspective, culture involves the transmission from generation to generation of specific ideas, arts, customary beliefs, ways of living, behavior patterns, institutions, and values. When the term *culture* is applied to the arts, it generally is used to specify "elite" kinds of artworks, such as operas, poetry, classical music, serious novels, and so on.

defense mechanisms   In Freud's psychoanalytic theory, *defense mechanisms* are methods used by the ego to defend itself against pressures from id, or impulsive elements in the psyche, and superego elements such as conscience and guilt. Some of the more common defense mechanisms are repression (barring unconscious instinctual wishes, memories, etc. from consciousness), regression (returning to earlier stages in one's development); ambivalence (a simultaneous feeling of love and hate for some person), and rationalization (offering excuses to justify one's actions).

demographics   *Demographics* refers to similarities found in selected groups of people, based on characteristics such as religion, gender, social class, ethnicity, occupation, place of residence, and age.

deviance   Individuals who are members of deviant groups have values and beliefs and behavior patterns that are different (that is, they deviate) from those of most people in society.

digital   "Digital systems," as Peter Lunenfeld explains things, "translate all input into binary structures of 0s and 1s, which can then be stored, transferred, or manipulated at the level or numbers of 'digits' (so called because etymologically, the word descends from the digits on our hand with which we count out those numbers)."

disfunctional (also dysfunctional)   Something is disfunctional if it contributes to the breakdown or destabilization of the entity in which it is found.

ego   In Freud's theory of the psyche, the *ego* functions as the executant of the id and as a mediator between the id and the superego. The ego is involved with the perception of reality and the adaptation to reality.

ethical criticism   Ethics is that branch of philosophy involving our sense of what is moral and correct. Ethical critics analyze texts based on the moral aspects of what happens in the texts as well as the possible impact of these texts on others.

ethnocentrism   *Ethnocentrism* refers to the notion held by some members of ethnic groups that their ideas, their customs, their beliefs, and their way of life are better than those held by other ethnic groups.

expressive theories of art   The expressive theory of art holds that the principal function of art is to express the feelings, beliefs, and emotions of the creator of texts and works of art.

false consciousness   For Marxists, *false consciousness* refers to mistaken ideas that members of the proletariat (and other classes as well) have about their class, status, and economic possibilities. These ideas help maintain the status quo and are of great use to the ruling class, which wants to avoid changes in the social structure. Marx argued that the ideas of the ruling class are always the ruling ideas in society.

feminist criticism   Feminist criticism, generally speaking, focuses on the roles given to women in texts and the way they are portrayed in general in texts of all kinds, but especially mass mediated ones. Feminist critics argue that women are typically used as sexual objects and are portrayed stereotypically in texts, and these perspectives have negative effects not only on women but also on men.

focal points   The term *focal points* refers to the five general topics or subject areas we can concentrate upon in dealing with mass communication. These are the work of art or text, the artist, the audience, America or the society, and the media.

formula In narrative theory, a formulaic text refers to a text with conventional characters and actions that audiences are familiar with. Genre texts—such as westerns, sitcoms, detective stories, science-fiction adventures, and romances—are highly formulaic.

functional In sociological theory, the term *functional* refers, broadly speaking, to the contribution an institution makes to the maintenance of society. Something is functional if it helps maintain the system in which it is found.

functional alternative The term *functional alternative* refers to an entity that can be used as an alternative to something—that is, it takes the place of something else. For example, professional football games can be seen as a functional alternative to religious services on Sundays.

gatekeepers Literally speaking, gatekeepers stand at some gate and determine who or what goes through it. In the news world, gatekeepers are editors and others who determine what stories are used in newspapers or news programs on the electronic media. Thus, these gatekeepers determine what news stories we get; but in a broader sense, gatekeepers decide what programs and films we see, what songs we hear, and so on.

gender *Gender* refers to the sexual category of an individual (masculine or feminine), and to behavioral traits customarily connected with each category.

genre *Genre* is a French word meaning "kind" or "class." In this book it refers to the kind of formulaic texts found in the mass media: soap operas, news shows, sport programs, horror shows, detective programs, and so on.

hypodermic needle theory of media The hypodermic theory, generally discredited now, holds that all members of an audience "read" a text the same way and get the same things out of it. Media is compared to a hypodermic needle, injecting its message to one and all. Some theorists talk about interpretive communities, which suggest that groups of people can get similar messages from texts. Here, "hypodermic needle" is used as a metaphor to characterize the way the media work.

hypothesis A hypothesis is a notion that is assumed to be true for the purposes of discussion or argument or further investigation. It is, in a sense, a guess or supposition that is used to explain some phenomenon.

id In Freud's theory of the psyche (technically known as his structural hypothesis), the *id* is that element of the psyche that is the representative of a person's drives. Freud called it, in *New Introductory Lectures on Psychoanalysis,* "a chaos, a cauldron of seething excitement." The id is also the source of energy; but lacking direction, it needs the ego to harness and control it. In popular thought, id is connected with impulse, lust, "I want it all now" kind of behavior.

ideology An ideology can be understood to mean a logically coherent, integrated explanation of social, economic, and political matters that helps establish the goals and direct the actions of some group or political entity. People act (and vote or don't vote) based on some ideology they hold, even though they may not have articulated it or thought much about it.

image   Defining *image* is extremely complicated. I define an image as a combination of signs and symbols—what we find when we look at a photograph, a film still, a shot of a television screen, a print advertisement, or just about anything. The term is also used for mental as well as physical representations of things. Images often have powerful emotional effects on people—and historical significance, as my discussion of 9/11 demonstrates. Two recent books that deal with images in some detail are Kiku Adatto's *Picture Perfect: The Art and Artifice of Public Image Making* and Paul Messaris's *Visual Literacy: Image, Mind and Reality.*

intertextuality   This term involves alluding to, imitating, adapting, and modifying previously created texts, styles of expression, or genres.

latent functions   Latent functions are understood to be hidden, unrecognized, and unintended functions of some activity, entity, or institution. They are contrasted by social scientists with manifest functions, which are recognized and intended.

lifestyles   Literally meaning "style of life," this term refers, loosely, to the way people live—to the decisions they make about such matters as how to decorate their apartment or home (and where it is located), what kind of car they drive, what kind of clothes to wear, what kinds of foods to eat (and which restaurants they dine at), where they go for vacations, and so on.

limited effects (of media)   Some mass communication theorists argue that the mass media have limited or relatively minor effects in the scheme of things. They cite research showing, for example, that effects from media don't tend to be long-lasting; and they argue that the notion that mass media have strong effects has not been demonstrated. This notion is no longer as prominent as it once was.

manifest functions   The manifest functions of some activity, entity, or institution are those that are obvious and intended. Manifest functions contrast with latent functions, which are hidden and unintended. The manifest function of television viewing may be for entertainment, while the latent function might involve becoming more materialistic.

mass   For our purposes, *mass,* as in "mass communication," refers to a large number of people who are the audience for some communication. There is considerable disagreement about how to understand the term *mass.* In earlier years, theorists said a mass is comprised of individuals who are heterogeneous, do not know one another, are alienated, and do not have a leader. Others attack these notions, saying they are not based on fact or evidence but on speculative theories that have not been verified.

mass communication *Mass communication* refers to the transfer of messages, information, texts, and so on from a sender of some kind to a large number of people, a mass audience. This transfer is done through the technologies of the mass media—newspapers, magazines, television programs, films, records, computers and CD ROMs, and so on. The sender often is a person in some large media organization, the messages are public, and the audience tends to be large and varied.

mass culture This theory suggests the mass media will create a mass society/ mass culture in which everyone would become a slave-like mass man or mass woman, alienated from others and easily manipulated.

media aesthetics When applied to the media, aesthetics involves the way technical matters such as lighting, sound, music, kinds of shots and camera work, and editing and related matters in texts affect the way members of audiences react to these texts.

media violence According to Gerbner and Signorelli, *media violence* can be defined as "the depiction of overt physical action that hurts or kills or threatens to do so" (1988: xi). In my discussion of violence, I offer varying kinds and aspects of violence that have to be considered in dealing with media portrayals of violence.

medium (plural: media) A *medium* is understood to be a means of delivering messages, information, and texts to audiences. Although there are different ways of classifying the media, here is one of the most common: print (newspapers, magazines, books, billboards), electronic (radio, television, computers, CD-ROMS), and photographic (photographs, films, videos). Other ways of classifying the media are described in this book.

metaphor A *metaphor* (Greek for "transfer") is a figure of speech that conveys meaning by analogy. We must realize that metaphors are not confined to poetry and literary works but, according to some linguists, are the fundamental ways in which we make sense of things and find meaning in the world. A *simile* is a weak form of metaphor (transferring meaning) that uses the word *like* or *as* in comparing things. Metaphors can be communicated by visual images; they aren't dependent upon language.

metonymy According to linguists, metonomy is a figure of speech that conveys information by association, and is, along with metaphor, one of the most important ways people convey information to one another. We tend not to be aware of our use of metonymy, but whenever we use association to get an idea about something (Rolls Royce = Wealthy), we are thinking metonymically. A form of metonymy that involves seeing a whole in terms of a part or vice versa is called *synecdoche*. Using "The White House" to stand for the presidency is an example of synecdoche. Like metaphors, metonymies can be communicated visually, using images.

mimetic theory of art   This theory, dating from Aristotle's time, suggests that art is an *imitation* of reality. Art, then, is a "mirror" of life, which explains why we can find so much about society and people in texts. Some theorists hold that art is not a mirror but a lamp that projects the reality of the creators behind texts.

model   In the social sciences, models are abstract representations that show how some phenomenon functions. Theories are typically expressed in language, but models tend to be represented graphically and often use statistics or mathematics. Denis McQuail and Sven Windahl define *model* in *Communication Models for the Study of Mass Communication* as "a consciously simplified description in graphic form of a piece of reality. A model seeks to show the main elements of any structure or process and the relationships between these elements" (1993: 2).

modernism   *Modernism* is the term used by critics in referring to the arts (architecture, literature, visual arts, dance, music, and so on) in the period from approximately the turn of the twentieth century until around the sixties. The modernists rejected narrative structure for simultaneity and montage and explored the paradoxical nature of reality. Some important modernists were T. S. Eliot, Franz Kafka, James Joyce, Pablo Picasso, Henri Matisse, and Eugene Ionesco. The period after modernism is called postmodernism.

narrowcasting   A medium like radio, which has stations that tend to focus on discrete groups of people, is said to be narrowcasting. This contrasts with broadcasting media, like television, which try to reach as large an audience as possible.

nonverbal communication   A great deal of communication comes from nonverbal phenomena. Our body language, facial expressions, style of dress, style of wearing our hair, and so on are examples of our communicating feelings and attitudes (and a sense of who we are) without using words. Even in conversations, a great deal of the communication comes from our body language.

phallic symbol   An object that resembles either by shape or function the penis is described as a phallic symbol. Symbolism is a defense mechanism of the ego that permits hidden or repressed sexual or aggressive thoughts to be expressed in a disguised form. For a discussion of this topic see Freud's book, *The Interpretation of Dreams*. Many print advertisements and television commercials make use of phallic symbols to excite people emotionally.

political cultures   According to the late political scientist Aaron Wildavsky, all democratic societies have four political cultures and need these four cultures to balance off one another. Wildavsky identified the four political cultures as individualists, elitists, egalitarians, and fatalists. A political culture is made up of people with similar political values and beliefs—and for Wildavsky, who observe similar group boundaries, rules, and prescriptions.

popular The word *popular* is one of the most difficult terms used in discourse about the arts and the media. Literally speaking, *popular* means "appealing to large numbers of people." It comes from the Latin word *popularis*, "of the people."

popular culture *Popular culture* is a term used in identifying certain kinds of mass mediated texts that appeal to large numbers of people—that is, that are popular. But mass communication theorists often identify (or should we say confuse) "popular" with "mass" and suggest that if something is popular, it must, by necessity, be of poor quality, appealing to the mythical lowest common denominator. Popular culture is generally held to be the opposite of "elite" culture—arts which require certain levels of sophistication and refinement to be appreciated, such as ballet, opera, poetry, classical music, and so on. Postmodern theorists reject this popular culture/elite culture polarity.

pornography Pornography is almost impossible to define. Generally speaking, pornography is held to be material that is sexually explicit and is meant to arouse sexual excitement. The root of the term, *porne*, means "prostitute" in Greek.

postmodernism We Americans are, some theorists suggest, living in a postmodern era—and we have been since the 1960s, more or less. Literally speaking, the term *postmodernism* (sometimes written as post-modernism) means "after modernism"—the period from approximately 1900 to the 1960s. Postmodernism is characterized by—as a leading theorist of the subject, Jean-François Lyotard, put it—"incredulity toward metanarratives" (*The Postmodern Condition: A Report on Knowledge,* 1984: xxiv). By this he means that the old philosophical belief systems or metanarratives that had helped people order their lives and societies no longer are accepted or given credulity. This leads to a period in which, some have suggested, anything goes.

power Power is, politically speaking, the ability to implement one's wishes as far as policy in some entity is concerned. When we use the term to discuss texts, we use it to describe their ability to have an emotional impact upon people—readers, viewers, or listeners—and sometimes to have social, economic, and political consequences.

psychoanalytic theory Freud's psychoanalytic theory is based on the notion that the human psyche has what he called an "unconscious," which (unlike consciousness and the preconscious) ordinarily speaking is inaccessible to individuals and continually shapes and affects our mental functioning and behavior. We can symbolize this concept by applying a metaphor. Imagine an iceberg; the tip of the iceberg, showing above the water, represents consciousness. The part of the iceberg we can see just below the water surface represents the preconscious. And the rest of the iceberg (most of it, which cannot be seen but we know it is there) represents the unconscious. We cannot access this area of our psyches because of repression. Freud also emphasized matters such as sexuality and the role of the Oedipus complex in everyone's lives and in our social relations.

psychographics   In marketing, *psychographics* is used in referring to groups of people who have similar psychological characteristics or profiles. The VALS (Values and Life Styles) typology is an example of a marketing system based on psychographics. Psychographics differs from demographics, which marketers use to focus upon social and economic characteristics that some people have in common.

public   Instead of the term *popular culture,* some theorists use phrases like "the public arts" or "public communication" to avoid the negative connotations of the terms *mass* and *popular.* A *public* is a group of people, a community. We can contrast public acts—those meant to be known to the community—with private acts, which are not meant to be known to others. But private acts often have social and public consequences.

rationalization   In Freudian thought, a *rationalization* is a defense mechanism of the ego that creates an excuse to justify some action (or inaction when an action is expected). Ernest Jones, who introduced the term, used it to describe logical and rational reasons that people give to justify behavior that is really caused by unconscious and irrational determinants.

reader response theory (also reception theory)   Reader response theory suggests that readers (a term used very broadly to cover people who read books, watch television programs, go to films, and listen to texts on the radio) play an important role in the realization of texts. Texts, then, function as sites for the creation of meaning by readers, and different readers interpret a given text differently. How differently is a matter of considerable conjecture.

relativism   In philosophical thought, *relativism* refers to the belief that truth is relative and not absolute; that there are no universally accepted objective standards. In ethical thought, relativism suggests there are no absolutes of morality and ethics. Thus, for relativists, different cultures have different ways of living and practices that are as valid as any others. That is, morality and ethical behavior are relative to particular groups and cannot be generalized to include all human beings. This contrasts with the notion that there are ethical absolutes or universals—which can and should be applied to everyone.

role A *role,* as sociologists use the term, is a way of behavior that we learn in a given society and that is held to be appropriate to a particular situation. A person generally plays many roles with different people during a given day, such as husband (marriage), parent (family), and worker (job).

secondary modeling systems Language, according to Yuri Lotman, is our primary modeling system. Works of art, which use phenomena such as myths and legends, function as secondary modeling systems; they are secondary to language, that is.

selective attention (or selective inattention) People have a tendency to avoid messages that conflict with their beliefs and values. One way people do this is by selective attention—by avoiding or not paying attention to messages that would generate cognitive dissonance.

semiotics Literally, *semiotics* means "the science of signs." *Sēmeîon* is the Greek word for "sign." A sign is anything that can be used to stand for anything else. According to C. S. Peirce, one of the founders of the science, a sign "is something which stands to somebody for something in some respect or capacity."

serial texts We refer to texts that continue for long periods of time as *serial texts.* Good examples would be comic strips, soap operas, and other television narratives that are on for extended periods of time. Serial texts pose problems for critics: What is the text, and how do we deal with it?

sign In semiotic theory, a *sign* is a combination of a *signifier* (sound, object) and a *signified* (concept). The relationship between the signifier and signified is arbitrary, based on convention. Signs are anything that can be used to stand for something else.

socioeconomic class *Socioeconomic class* is a categorization of people according to their incomes and related social status and lifestyles. In Marxist thought, there are ruling classes that shape the consciousness of the working classes; and history is, in essence, a record of class conflict.

social controls *Social controls* are the ideas, beliefs, values, and mores people get from their societies that shape their beliefs and behavior. People are not only individuals, with certain distinctive physical and emotional characteristics and desires, but also—at the same time—members of societies, as Emile Durkheim pointed out. And people are shaped, to a certain degree, by the institutions found in these societies.

socialization *Socialization* refers to the processes by which societies teach individuals how to behave, that is, what rules to obey, what roles to assume, and what values to hold. Socialization was traditionally done by the family, by educators, by religious figures, and by peers. The mass media seem to have usurped this function to a considerable degree nowadays, with consequences that are not always positive. Anthropologists use the term *enculturation* to indicate the process by which an individual is taught cultural values and practices.

society   A society is a human group that is self-perpetuating, that occupies a territory and shares a culture. It is independent, and most associations are within the group.

spiral of silence   This theory, developed by German scholar Elizabeth Noelle-Neuman, argues that people who hold views that they think are not widely held (whether this is correct or not) tend to keep quiet, while those who hold views that they believe are widely accepted tend to state their views strongly. Together, these attitudes lead to a spiral in which certain views tend to be suppressed while others gain increased prominence.

stereotypes   Commonly held, simplistic, and inaccurate group portraits of categories of people are called *stereotypes*. These stereotypes can have a positive, negative, or mixed viewpoint; but they are usually negative. Stereotyping always involves making gross overgeneralizations. (All Mexicans; or all Chinese; or all Jews; or all lawyers, doctors, professors, and so on are held to have certain characteristics.)

subculture   Subcultures are cultural subgroups whose religious practices, ethnicity, sexual orientation, beliefs, values, behaviors, and lifestyles vary in certain ways from those of the dominant mainstream culture. In any complex society, it is normal to have a considerable number of subcultures.

subliminal   This concept suggests that images shown on television or film screens for only a small fraction of a second and generally not consciously recognized by viewers can have effects on people exposed to these images.

superego   In Freud's theory of the psyche, the *superego* is the agency in our psyches related to conscience and morality. The superego is involved with processes such as approval and disapproval of wishes on the basis of their morality, with critical self-observation, and with experiencing a sense of guilt over wrongdoing. The functions of the superego are largely unconscious, and are opposed to id elements in our psyches. Mediating between the two, and trying to balance them, are our egos.

text   The term *text* is used in academic discourse to refer, broadly speaking, to any work of art in any medium. Critics use the word *text* as a convenience, so they don't have to name a given work all the time or use various synonyms. There are problems involved in deciding what the text is when we deal with serial texts, such as soap operas or comics.

theory   A *theory,* as the term is conventionally understood, is expressed in language and systematically and logically attempts to explain and predict phenomena being studied. Theories differ from concepts, which define phenomena that are being studied, and from models, which are abstract, usually graphic in nature, and explicit about what is being studied.

typology A *typology* is a classification scheme or system of categories that someone uses to make sense of some phenomena. Classification schemes are important because the way we classify things affects the way we think about them.

Ur-text An Ur-text is a template for other texts, a foundational model from which other texts are derived.

uses and gratifications The uses and gratifications theory argues that researchers should pay attention to the way members of audiences use the media (or certain texts or genres of texts) and the gratifications they get from their use of these texts and the media. Uses and gratifications researchers focus, then, on how audiences use the media and not on how the media affect audiences.

values *Values* are understood to be abstract and general beliefs or judgments about what is right and wrong, what is good and bad, with implications for individual behavior and for social, cultural, and political entities. From a philosophical point of view, there are a number of problems with values. First, how does one determine which values are correct or good and which aren't? That is, how do we justify values? Are values objective or subjective? Second, what happens when there is a conflict between groups, each of which holds a central value conflicting with that of a different group?

video games Video games are electronic games that are interactive—that is, they allow players to participate in the action of the game. They are played, generally speaking, on specialized consoles with powerful graphic and sound capabilities, though many video games can also be played on computers.

violence (mass mediated) *See* media violence.

youth culture *Youth cultures* are subcultures formed by young people around some area of interest, usually connected with leisure and entertainment—for example, surfing, skateboarding, rock music, or some aspect of computers (games, hacking, and so on). Typically, members of youth cultures adopt distinctive ways of dressing and develop institutions that cater to their needs.

SELECT BIBLIOGRAPHY

Adatto, Kiku. 1993. *Picture Perfect: The Art and Artifice of Public Image Making.* New York: Basic Books.

Adorno, Theodor W. 1967. *Prisms.* Trans. Samuel and Sherry Weber. Cambridge: MIT Press.

———. 1991. *The Culture Industry: Selected Essays on Mass Culture.* London: Routledge.

Anders, Gunther. 1957. "The Phantom World of TV." In Bernard Rosenberg and David Manning White, eds. *Mass Culture: The Popular Arts in America.* New York: Free Press.

Armstrong, Nancy. 1987. *Desire and Domestic Fiction: A Political History of the Novel.* New York: Oxford University Press.

Aronowitz, Stanley. 1992. *The Politics of Identity.* New York: Routledge.

———. 1993. *Dead Artists, Live Theories and Other Cultural Problems.* New York: Routledge.

Bagdikian, Ben H. 2000. *The Media Monopoly* (6th ed.). Boston: Beacon Press.

Bakhtin, Mikhail M. 1981. *The Dialogic Imagination.* Trans. Caryl Emerson and Michael Holmquist; ed. Michael Holmquist. Austin: University of Texas Press.

———. 1984. *Rabelais and His World.* Trans. Helene Iswolsky. Bloomington: Indiana University Press.

Bal, Mieke. 1985. *Narratology: Introduction to the Theory of Narrative.* Toronto: University of Toronto Press.

Barker, Martin, and Ann Beezer. 1992. *Reading into Cultural Studies.* London: Routledge.

Barthes, Roland. 1970. *Writing Degree Zero & Elements of Semiology.* Trans. Annette Lavers and Colin Smith. Boston: Beacon Press.

————. 1972. *Mythologies*. Trans. Annette Lavers. New York: Hill and Wang.

————. 1977. *Empire of Signs*. Trans. Stephen Heath. New York: Hill and Wang.

————. 1988. *The Semiotic Challenge*. Trans. Richard Howard. New York: Hill and Wang.

Bateson, Gregory. 1972. *Steps to an Ecology of Mind*. New York: Ballantine Books.

Baudrillard, Jean. 1983. *Simulations*. Trans. Paul Foss et al. New York: Semiotext(e).

————. 1996. *The System of Objects*. Trans. James Benedict. London: Verso.

Beilharz, Peter, Gillian Robinson, and John Rundell. 1992. *Between Totalitarianism and Postmodernity: A Thesis Eleven Reader*. Cambridge, Mass.: MIT Press.

Bennett, Tony, and Janet Woollacott. 1987. *Bond and Beyond: The Political Career of a Popular Hero*. New York: Methuen.

Berger, Arthur Asa. 1973. *The Comic-Stripped American*. New York: Walker & Co.

————. 1975. *The TV-Guided American*. New York: Walker & Co.

————. 1984. *Signs in Contemporary Culture: An Introduction to Semiotics*. New York: Annenberg-Longman.

————. 1989. *Seeing Is Believing: An Introduction to Visual Communication*. Mountain View, Calif.: Mayfield.

————. 1990. *Agitpop: Political Culture and Communication Theory*. New Brunswick, N.J.: Transaction.

————, ed. 1991. *Media USA: Process and Effect* (2d ed.). New York: Longman.

————. 1993. *An Anatomy of Humor*. New Brunswick, N.J.: Transaction.

————. 1994. *Blind Men and Elephants: Perspectives on Humor*. New Brunswick, N.J.: Transaction.

————. 1994. *Cultural Criticism: A Primer of Key Concepts*. Thousand Oaks, Calif.: Sage Publications.

————. 1997. *Postmortem for a Postmodernist*. Walnut Creek, Calif.: AltaMira Press.

————, ed. 1998. *The Postmodern Presence: Readings on Postmodernism in American Culture and Society*. Walnut Creek, Calif.: AltaMira Press.

————. 1998. *Media Analysis Techniques* (2d ed.). Thousand Oaks, Calif.: Sage Publications.

————. 2000. *Ads, Fads and Consumer Culture*. Boulder, Colo.: Rowman & Littlefield.

————. 2001. *Jewish Jesters*. Cresskill, N.J.: Hampton Press.

————. 2002. *The Mass Comm Murders: Five Media Theorists Self-Destruct*. Lanham, Md.: Rowman & Littlefield.

———. 2002. *Video Games: A Popular Culture Phenomenon.* New Brunswick, N.J.: Transaction.

Berman, Marshall. 1982. *All That Is Solid Melts into Air: The Experience of Modernity.* New York: Touchstone Books.

Best, Steven, and Douglas Kellner. 1991. *Postmodern Theory.* New York: Guilford.

Bettelheim, Bruno. 1976. *The Uses of Enchantment.* New York: Knopf.

Blau, Herbert. 1992. *To All Appearances: Ideology and Performance.* London: Routledge.

Bogart, Leo. 1985. *Polls and the Awareness of Public Opinion.* New Brunswick, N.J.: Transaction.

Bolter, Jay David, and Richard Grusin. 2000. *Remediation: Understanding New Media.* Cambridge, Mass.: MIT Press.

Boorstin, Daniel. 1975. *The Image: A Guide to Pseudo-Events in America.* New York: Atheneum.

Bowlby, Rachel. 1993. *Shopping with Freud: Items on Consumerism, Feminism and Psychoanalysis.* London: Routledge.

Brenkman. 1993. *Straight Male Modern: A Cultural Critique of Psychoanalysis.* New York: Routledge.

Brenner, Charles. 1974. *An Elementary Textbook of Psychoanalysis.* Garden City, N.Y.: Anchor Books.

Brown, Mary Ellen, ed. 1990. *Television and Women's Culture: The Politics of the Popular.* Newbury Park, Calif.: Sage Publications.

———. 1994. *Soap Opera and Woman's Talk: The Pleasure of Resistance.* Thousand Oaks, Calif.: Sage Publications.

Buck-Morss, Susan. 1989. *The Dialectics of Seeing: Walter Benjamin and the Arcades Project.* Minneapolis: University of Minnesota Press.

Burton, Graeme. 1990. *More Than Meets the Eye: An Introduction to Media Studies.* London: Arnold.

Butler, Judith. 1993. *Bodies That Matter.* New York: Routledge.

Cantor, Muriel G. 1988. *The Hollywood TV Producer.* New Brunswick, N.J.: Transaction.

Cantor, Muriel G., and Joel M. Cantor. 1991. *Prime-Time Television: Content and Control.* Thousand Oaks, Calif.: Sage Publications.

Carey, James, ed. 1988. *Media, Myths and Narratives: Television and the Press.* Newbury Park, Calif.: Sage Publications.

Cawelti, John. 1971. *The Six-Gun Mystique.* Bowling Green, Ohio: Bowling Green Popular Press.

Certeau, Michel de. 1984. *The Practice of Everyday Life.* Trans. Steven Rendall. Berkeley: University of California Press.

————. 1986. *Heterologies: Discourse on the Other.* Trans. Brian Massumi. Minneapolis: University of Minnesota Press

Clarke, John. 1992. *New Times and Old Enemies: Essays on Cultural Studies and America.* London: Routledge.

Cohen, Jodi R. 1998. *Communication Criticism: Developing Your Critical Powers.* Thousand Oaks, Calif.: Sage Publications.

Collins, Richard, James Curran, Nicholas Garnham, and Paddy Scannell, eds. 1986. *Media, Culture & Society: A Critical Reader.* Newbury Park, Calif.: Sage Publications.

Cortese, Anthony J. 1999. *Images of Women and Minorities in Advertising.* Boulder, Colo.: Rowman & Littlefield.

Coward, Rosalind, and John Ellis. 1977. *Language and Materialism: Developments in Semiology and the Theory of the Subject.* London: Routledge & Kegan Paul.

Crane, Diane. 1992. *The Production of Culture: Media and the Urban Arts.* Newbury Park, Calif.: Sage Publications.

Creed, Barbara. 1993. *The Monstrous-Feminine: Film, Feminism, Psychoanalysis.* London: Routledge.

Creedon, Pamela J. 1993. *Women in Mass Communication* (2d ed.). Thousand Oaks, Calif.: Sage Publications.

Croce, Paul Jerome. 1992. "The Polarization of America: The Decline of Mass Culture." *The Public Perspective,* September–October.

Crook, Stephen, Jan Pakulski, and Malcolm Waters, eds. 1992. *Postmodernization: Change in Advanced Society.* London: Sage Publications.

Cross, Gary. 1993. *Time and Money: The Making of a Consumer Culture.* London: Routledge.

Culler, Jonathan. 1976. *Structuralist Poetics: Structuralism, Linguistics and the Study of Literature.* Ithaca, N.Y.: Cornell University Press.

————. 1977. *Ferdinand de Saussure.* New York: Penguin Books.

————. 1981. *The Pursuit of Signs.* Ithaca, N.Y.: Cornell University Press.

————. 1982. *On Deconstruction.* Ithaca, N.Y.: Cornell University Press.

Danesi, Marcel. 1994. *Messages and Meanings: An Introduction to Semiotics.* Toronto: Canadian Scholars Press.

————. 2002. *Understanding Media Semiotics.* London: Arnold.

Danesi, Marcel, and Donato Santeramo, eds. 1992. *Introducing Semiotics: An Anthology of Readings.* Toronto: Canadian Scholars Press.

Davis, Robert Con, and Ronald Schleifer. 1991. *Criticism & Culture.* London: Longman.

Denney, Reuel. 1989. *The Astonished Muse.* New Brunswick, N.J.: Transaction.

Denzin, Norman K. 1991. *Images of Postmodern Society: Social Theory and Contemporary Cinema.* London: Sage Publications.

De Tocqueville, Alexis. 1956. *Democracy in America*. New York: Mentor Books.

Doane, Mary Ann. 1991. *Femmes Fatales*. New York: Routledge.

Donald, James, and Stuart Hall, eds. 1985. *Politics and Ideology*. Bristol, Pa.: Taylor & Francis.

Douglas, Mary. 1975. *Implicit Meanings: Essays in Anthropology*. London: Routledge & Kegan Paul.

———. 1992. *Risk and Blame: Essays in Cultural Theory*. London: Routledge.

Duncan, Hugh Dalziel. 1985. *Communication and the Social Order*. New Brunswick, N.J.: Transaction.

Dundes, Alan. 1987. *Cracking Jokes: Studies in Sick Humor Cycles and Stereotypes*. Berkeley, Calif.: Ten Speed Press.

Durkheim, Emile. 1967. *The Elementary Forms of the Religious Life*. New York: Free Press.

Dyer, Richard. 1993. *The Matter of Images: Essays on Representations*. London: Routledge.

Eagleton, Terry. 1976. *Marxism and Literary Criticism*. Berkeley: University of California Press.

———. 1983. *Literary Theory: An Introduction*. Minneapolis: University of Minnesota Press.

Easthope, Antony. 1991. *Literary into Cultural Studies*. London: Routledge.

Eco, Umberto. 1972. "Towards a Semiotic Inquiry into the Television Message." *Working Papers in Cultural Studies* 3 (Autumn).

———. 1976. *A Theory of Semiotics*. Bloomington: Indiana University Press.

———. 1984. *The Role of the Reader*. Bloomington: Indiana University Press.

Elam, Keir. 1980. *The Semiotics of Theatre and Drama*. London: Methuen.

Esslin, Martin. 1982. *The Age of Television*. San Francisco: W.H. Freeman.

Ettema, James S., and D. Charles Whitney, eds. 1994. *Audiencemaking: How the Media Create the Audience*. Thousand Oaks, Calif.: Sage Publications.

Ewen, Stuart. 1976. *Captains of Consciousness*. New York: McGraw-Hill.

Ewen, Stuart, and Elizabeth Ewen. 1982. *Channels of Desire: Mass Images and the Shaping of American Consciousness*. New York: McGraw-Hill.

Featherstone, Mike. 1991. *Consumer Culture & Postmodernism*. London: Sage Publications.

Fiske, John. 1989. *Reading the Popular*. London: Routledge.

———. 1989. *Understanding Popular Culture*. London: Routledge.

Fiske, John, and John Hartley. 1978. *Reading Television*. London: Methuen & Co.

Fjellman, Stephen M. 1992. *Vinyl Leaves: Walt Disney World and America*. Boulder, Colo.: Westview.

Franklin, Sarah, Celia Lury, and Jackie Stacey. 1992. *Off-Centre: Feminism and Cultural Studies*. London: Routledge.

Freud, Sigmund. 1960. *A General Introduction to Psychoanalysis.* Trans. Joan Riviere. New York: Washington Square Press.

———. 1963. *Jokes and Their Relation to the Unconscious.* Trans. James Strachey. New York: Norton.

———. 1965. *The Interpretation of Dreams.* Trans. James Strachey. New York: Avon.

Friedson, Elliot. 1953. "Communication Research and the Concept of the Mass." *American Sociological Review* 18.

Frith, Simon. 1981. *Sound Effects: Youth, Leisure and the Politics of Rock and Roll.* New York: Pantheon.

Fry, William F. 1968. *Sweet Madness: A Study of Humor.* Palo Alto, Calif.: Pacific Books.

Gandelman, Claude. 1991. *Reading Pictures, Viewing Texts.* Bloomington: Indiana University Press.

Garber, Marjorie. 1993. *Vested Interests: Cross-Dressing and Cultural Anxiety.* New York: HarperPerennial.

Garber, Marjorie, Jann Matlock, and Rebecca Walkowtiz, eds. 1993. *Media Spectacles.* New York: Routledge.

Garber, Marjorie, Pratibha Parmar, and John Greyson, eds. 1993. *Queer Looks: Perspectives on Lesbian and Gay Film and Video.* New York: Routledge.

Gee, James Paul. 2003. *What Video Games Have to Teach Us about Learning and Literacy.* New York: Palgrave-Macmillan.

Gerbner, George, and Nancy Signorelli. 1988. *Violence and Terror in the Mass Media: An Annotated Bibliography.* Westport, Conn.: Greenwood Press.

Gitlin, Todd. 1985. *Inside Prime Time.* New York: Pantheon.

Goldstein, Ann, Mary Jane Jacob, Anne Rimer, and Howard Singerman. 1989. *A Forest of Signs: Art in the Crisis of Representation.* Cambridge, Mass.: MIT Press.

Greenblatt, Stephen J. 1992. *Learning to Curse: Essays in Early Modern Culture.* New York: Routledge.

Greenfield, Lauren. 2002. *Girl Culture.* San Francisco: Chronicle Books.

Greenfield, Patricia Marks. 1984. *Mind and Media: The Effects of Television, Video Games, and Computers.* Cambridge, Mass.: Harvard University Press.

Grossberg, Lawrence. 1992. *We Gotta Get Out of This Place: Popular Conservatism and Postmodern Culture.* New York: Routledge.

Grossberg, Lawrence, Cary Nelson, and Paula Treicher. 1991. *Cultural Studies.* New York: Routledge.

Grotjahn, Martin. 1966. *Beyond Laughter: Humor and the Subconscious.* New York: McGraw-Hill.

Guiraud, Pierre. 1975. *Semiology.* London: Routledge & Kegan Paul.

Gumbrecht, Hans Ulrich. 1992. *Making Sense in Life and Literature.* Trans. Glen Burns. Minneapolis: University of Minnesota Press.

Habermas, Jürgen. 1987. *The Philosophical Discourse of Modernity: Twelve Lectures.* Trans. Frederick G. Lawrence. Minneapolis: University of Minnesota Press.

———. 1989. *The New Conservatism: Cultural Criticism and the Historians' Debate.* Trans. Sherry Weber Nicholsen. Minneapolis: University of Minnesota Press.

Hall, Stuart. 1988. *The Hard Road to Renewal.* London: Verso.

———. 1991. *New Times: The Changing Face of Politics in the 1990s.* London: Routledge.

Hall, Stuart, and Tony Jefferson, eds. 1990. *Resistance through Rituals: Youth Sub-cultures in Postwar Britain.* London: Routledge. (This was originally published as *Working Papers in Cultural Studies* 7/8 from the Centre for Contemporary Cultural Studies at the University of Birmingham [Birmingham, UK]. For an in-depth study of Stuart Hall's work, see *Journal of Communication Inquiry* [Summer 1986], which is devoted to him.)

Hall, Stuart, and Paddy Whannel. 1967. *The Popular Arts: A Critical Guide to the Mass Media.* Boston: Beacon Press.

Hartley, John. 1992. *The Politics of Pictures: The Creation of the Public in the Age of Popular Media.* London: Routledge.

———. 1992. *Tele-ology: Studies in Television.* London: Routledge.

Haug, W. F. 1971. *Critique of Commodity Aesthetics: Appearance, Sexuality and Advertising in Capitalist Society.* Trans. Robert Bock. Minneapolis: University of Minnesota Press.

———. 1987. *Commodity Aesthetics, Ideology & Culture.* New York: International General.

Herzog, Herta. 1986. "Decoding Dallas," *Society,* p. 74.

Hoggart, Richard. 1992. *The Uses of Literacy.* New Brunswick, N.J.: Transaction.

Hoover, Stewart M. 1988. *Mass Media Religion: The Social Sources of the Electronic Church.* Newbury Park, Calif.: Sage Publications.

Hutcheon, Linda. 1989. *The Politics of Postmodernism.* London: Routledge.

Iser, Wolfgang. 1988. "The Reading Process: A Phenomenological Approach." In D. Lodge ed., *Modern Criticism and Theory: A Reader.* White Plains, N.Y.: Longman.

Jacobs, Norman, ed. 1992. *Mass Media in Modern Society.* New Brunswick, N.J.: Transaction.

Jakobson, Roman. 1985. *Verbal Art, Verbal Sign, Verbal Time.* Eds. Krystyna Pomorska and Stephen Rudy. Minneapolis: University of Minnesota Press.

Jally, Sut, and Justin Lewis. 1992. *Enlightened Racism: The Cosby Show, Audiences and the Myth of the American Dream.* Boulder, Colo.: Westview.

Jameson, Frederic. 1981. *The Political Unconscious.* Ithaca, N.Y.: Cornell University Press.

———. 1991. *Postmodernism: Or the Cultural Logic of Late Capitalism.* Durham, N.C.: Duke University Press.

———. 1992. *The Geopolitical Aesthetic: Cinema and Space in the World System.* Bloomington: Indiana University Press.

———. 1992. *Signatures of the Visible.* New York: Routledge.

Jauss, Hans Robert. 1982. *Toward an Aesthetic of Reception.* Trans. Timothy Bahti. Minneapolis: University of Minnesota Press.

Jensen, Joli. 1990. *Redeeming Modernity: Contradictions in Media Criticism.* Newbury Park, Calif.: Sage Publications.

Jones, Steve. 1992. *Rock Formation: Music, Technology and Mass Communication.* Thousand Oaks, Calif.: Sage Publications.

———, ed. 1994. *Cybersociety: Computer-Mediated Communication and Community.* Thousand Oaks, Calif.: Sage Publications.

Jowett, Garth, and James M. Linton. 1989. *Movies as Mass Communication.* Newbury Park, Calif.: Sage Publications.

Jowett, Garth S., and Victoria O'Donnell. 1992. *Propaganda and Persuasion* (2d ed.). Thousand Oaks, Calif.: Sage Publications.

Jung, Carl G., ed. 1964. *Man and His Symbols.* New York: Dell.

Kamalipour, Yahya R., and Kuldip R. Rampal, eds. 2001. *Media, Sex, Violence, and Drugs in the Global Village.* Lanham, Md.: Rowman & Littlefield.

Kellner, Douglas. 1988. "Postmodernism as Social Theory: Some Challenges and Problems." *Theory, Culture & Society* 5, nos. 2–3 (June): 239.

———. 1992. *The Persian Gulf TV War.* Boulder, Colo.: Westview.

Kern, Montague. 1989. *30-Second Politics: Political Advertising in the Eighties.* New York: Praeger.

Korzenny, Felix, and Stella Ting-Toomey, eds. 1992. *Mass Media Effects across Cultures.* Newbury Park, Calif.: Sage Publications.

Lacan, Jacques. 1966. *Ecrits: A Selection.* Trans. Alan Sheridan. New York: Norton.

Laurentis, Teresa de. 1984. *Alice Doesn't: Feminism, Semiotics, Cinema.* Bloomington: Indiana University Press.

———. 1987. *Technologies of Gender: Essays on Theory, Film and Fiction.* Bloomington: Indiana University Press.

Lazere, Donald, ed. 1987. *America Media and Mass Culture: Left Perspectives.* Berkeley: University of California Press.

LeFebvre, Henri. 1984. *Everyday Life in the Modern World.* Trans. Sacha Rabinovitch. New Brunswick, N.J.: Transaction.

Lévi-Strauss, Claude. 1967. *Structural Anthropology.* Garden City, N.Y.: Doubleday.

Levy, Mark R., and Michael Gurevitch, eds. 1994. *Defining Media Studies: Reflections on the Future of the Field.* New York: Oxford University Press.

Lipsitz, George. 1989. *Time Passages: Collective Memory and American Popular Culture*. Minneapolis: University of Minnesota Press.

Lotman, Yuri M. 1976. *Semiotics of Cinema*. Ann Arbor: Michigan Slavic Contributions.

———. 1977. *The Structure of the Artistic Text*. Trans. Gail Lenhoff and Ronald Vroon. Ann Arbor: Michigan Slavic Contributions.

———. 1991. *Universe of the Mind: A Semiotic Theory of Culture*. Bloomington: Indiana University Press.

Lull, James. 1991. *Popular Music and Communication*. Thousand Oaks: Sage Publications.

Lunenfeld, Peter, ed. 1999. *The Digital Dialectic: New Essays on New Media*. Cambridge, Mass.: MIT Press.

Lunenfeld, Peter. 2000. *Snap to Grid: A User's Guide to Digital Arts, Media, and Cultures*. Cambridge, Mass.: MIT Press.

Lyotard, Jean-François. 1984. *The Postmodern Condition: A Report on Knowledge*. Minneapolis: University of Minnesota Press.

MacCannell, Dean, and Juliet Flower MacCannell. 1982. *The Time of the Sign: A Semiotic Interpretation of Modern Culture*. Bloomington: Indiana University Press.

MacDonald, J. Fred. 1994. *One Nation under Television*. Chicago: Nelson-Hall.

McCarthy, Thomas. 1991. *Ideals and Illusions: On Reconstruction and Deconstruction in Contemporary Critical Theory*. Cambridge, Mass.: MIT Press.

McCue, Greg, with Clive Bloom. 1993. *Dark Knights: The New Comics in Context*. Boulder, Colo.: Westview.

McLuhan, Marshall. 1965. *Understanding Media: The Extensions of Man*. New York: McGraw-Hill.

———. 1967. *The Mechanical Bride*. Boston: Beacon Press.

———. 1970. *Culture Is Our Business*. New York: McGraw-Hill.

McLuhan, Marshall, and Quentin Fiore. 1967. *The Medium Is the Massage*. New York: Bantam Books.

McQuail, Denis. 1992. *Media Performance: Mass Communication and the Public Interest*. Thousand Oaks, Calif.: Sage Publications.

———. 1994. *Mass Communication Theory: An Introduction* (3d ed.). Thousand Oaks, Calif.: Sage Publications.

McQuail, Denis, and Sven Windahl. 1993. *Communication Models for the Study of Mass Communication*. New York: Longman.

Mandel, Ernest. 1985. *Delightful Murder: A Social History of the Crime Story*. Minneapolis: University of Minnesota Press.

Mattelart, Armand, and Michele Mattelart. 1992. *Rethinking Media Theory*. Trans. James A. Cohen and Marina Urquidi. Minneapolis: University of Minnesota Press.

Mellencamp, Patricia. 1990. *Indiscretions: Avant-Garde Film, Video and Feminism.* Bloomington: Indiana University Press.

————, ed. 1990. *Logics of Television: Essays in Cultural Criticism.* Bloomington: Indiana University Press.

Messaris, Paul. 1994. *Visual Literacy: Image, Mind & Reality.* Boulder. Colo.: Westview.

Metz, Christian. 1982. *The Imaginary Signifier: Psychoanalysis and the Cinema.* Trans. Celia Britton et al. Bloomington: Indiana University Press.

Mindess, Harvey. 1971. *Laughter and Liberation.* Los Angeles: Nash Publishing.

Modleski, Tania. 1984. *Loving with a Vengeance: Mass-Produced Fantasies for Women.* New York: Routledge.

————. 1988. *The Women Who Knew Too Much: Hitchcock and Feminist Theory.* New York: Routledge.

————, ed. 1986. *Studies in Entertainment: Critical Approaches to Mass Culture.* Bloomington: Indiana University Press.

Moores, Shaun. 1994. *Interpreting Audiences: The Ethnography of Media Consumption.* Thousand Oaks, Calif.: Sage Publications.

Morley, David. 1988. *Family Television: Cultural Power and Domestic Leisure.* London: Routledge.

————. 1993. *Television Audiences and Cultural Studies.* London: Routledge.

Mulvey, Laura. 1989. *Visual and Other Pleasures.* Bloomington: Indiana University Press.

Nash, Christopher, ed. 1990. *Narrative in Culture.* London: Routledge.

Navarro, Desiderio, ed. 1993 (Summer). "Postmodernism: Center and Periphery." In *South Atlantic Quarterly.* Durham, N.C.: Duke University Press.

Nichols, Bill. 1981. *Ideology and the Image: Social Representation in the Cinema and Other Media.* Bloomington: Indiana University Press.

————. 1992. *Representing Reality: Issues and Concepts in Documentary.* Bloomington: Indiana University Press.

Noelle-Neumann, Elizabeth. 1974. "The Spiral of Silence: A Theory of Public Opinion." *Journal of Communication* 24(2), p. 44.

O'Shaugnessy, Michael. 2001. *Media and Society: An Introduction.* New York: Oxford University Press.

Peirce, C. S. 1958. *The Collected Papers of C. S. Peirce* (vols. 7–8). Ed. A. W. Burks. Cambridge: Harvard University Press.

Penley, Constance. 1989. *The Future of an Illusion: Film, Feminism and Psychoanalysis.* Minneapolis: University of Minnesota Press.

Phelan, James, ed. 1989. *Reading Narrative: Form, Ethics, Ideology.* Columbus: Ohio State University Press.

Potter, W. James. 1998. *Media Literacy.* Thousand Oaks: Sage Publications.

Powell, Chris, and George E. C. Paton, eds. 1988. *Humour in Society: Resistance and Control.* New York: St. Martin's Press.

Prindle, David. F. 1993. *Risky Business: The Political Economy of Hollywood.* Boulder, Colo.: Westview.

Propp, Vladimir. 1973. *Morphology of the Folk Tale* (2d ed.). Austin: University of Texas Press.

————. 1984. *Theory and History of Folklore.* Trans. Ariadna Y. Martin and Richard P. Martin. Minneapolis: University of Minnesota Press.

Ramet, Sabrina Petra, ed. 1993. *Rocking the State: Rock Music and Politics in Eastern Europe and the Soviet Union.* Boulder, Colo.: Westview.

Real, Michael R. 1989. *Supermedia: A Cultural Studies Approach.* Newbury Park, Calif.: Sage Publications.

————. 1996. *Exploring Media Culture: A Guide.* Thousand Oaks, Calif.: Sage Publications.

Reinelt, Janelle G., and Joseph R. Roach, eds. 1993. *Critical Theory and Performance.* Ann Arbor: University of Michigan Press.

Rheingold, Howard. 1991. *Virtual Reality.* New York: Summit Books.

Richardson Jr., Glenn W. 2003. *Pulp Politics: How Political Advertising Tells the Stories of American Politics.* Lanham, Md.: Rowman & Littlefield.

Richardson, Laurel. 1990. "Narrative and Sociology." *Journal of Contemporary Ethnology* 19: 118.

Richter, Mischa, and Harald Bakken. 1992. *The Cartoonist's Muse: A Guide to Generating and Developing Creative Ideas.* Chicago: Contemporary Books.

Rosenberg, Bernard, and David Manning White, eds. 1957. *Mass Culture: The Popular Arts in America.* New York: Free Press.

Ryan, John, and William M. Wentworth. 1998. *Media and Society: The Production of Culture in the Mass Media.* New York: Allyn & Bacon.

Ryan, Michael, and Douglas Kellner. 1988. *Camera Politica: The Politics and Ideology of Contemporary Hollywood Film.* Bloomington: Indiana University Press.

Sabin, Roger. 1993. *Adult Comics: An Introduction.* London: Routledge.

Saussure, Ferdinand de. 1966. *Course in General Linguistics.* Trans. Wade Baskin. New York: McGraw-Hill.

Schechner, Richard. 1993. *The Future of Ritual: Writings on Culture and Performance.* London: Routledge.

Scheuer, Jeffrey. 1999. *The Sound Bite Society: Television and the American Mind.* New York: Four Walls Eight Windows.

Schneider, Cynthia, and Brian Wallis, eds. 1989. *Global Television.* Cambridge, Mass.: MIT Press.

Schostak, John. 1993. *Dirty Marks: The Education of Self, Media and Popular Culture.* Boulder, Colo.: Westview.

Schwichtenberg, Cathy, ed. 1992. *The Madonna Collection.* Boulder, Colo.: Westview.

Seib, Philip. 2002. *Going Live: Getting the News Right in a Real-Time Online World*. Lanham, Md.: Rowman & Littlefield.

Skovman, Michael, ed. undated. *Media Fictions*. Aarhus, Denmark: Aarhus University Press.

Sebeok, Thomas, ed. 1978. *Sight, Sound and Sense*. Bloomington: Indiana University Press.

Seldes, Gilbert. 1994. *The Public Arts*. New Brunswick, N.J.: Transaction.

Sherman, Barry L. 1995. *Telecommunications Management: Broadcasting/Cable and the New Technologies* (2d ed.). New York: McGraw-Hill.

Shukman, Ann. 1977. *Literature and Semiotics: A Study of the Writings of Yuri M. Lotman*. Amsterdam: North Holland Publishing.

Silverman, Kaja. 1983. *The Subject of Semiotics*. New York: Oxford University Press.

Smith, Gary, ed. 1988. *On Walter Benjamin: Critical Essays and Recollections*. Cambridge, Mass.: MIT Press.

Steidman, Steven. 1993. *Romantic Longings: Love in America 1830–1980*. New York: Routledge.

Stephenson, William. 1988. *The Play Theory of Mass Communication*. New Brunswick, N.J.: Transaction.

Szondi, Peter. 1986. *On Textual Understanding*. Trans. Harvey Mendelsohn. Minneapolis: University of Minnesota Press.

Theall, Donald F. 2001. *The Virtual Marshall McLuhan*. Montreal and Kingston: McGill-Queen's University Press.

Todorov, Tzvetan. 1975. *The Fantastic: A Structural Approach to a Literary Genre*. Trans. Richard Howard. Ithaca, N.Y.: Cornell University Press.

———. 1981. *Introduction to Poetics*. Trans. Richard Howard. Minneapolis: University of Minnesota Press.

Traube, Elizabeth G. 1982. *Dreaming Identities: Class, Gender, and Generation in the 1980s Hollywood Movies*. Boulder, Colo.: Westview.

Turner, Bryan S. 1990. *Theories of Modernity and Postmodernity*. London: Sage Publications.

Van Zoonen, Liesbet. 1994. *Feminist Media Studies*. Thousand Oaks, Calif.: Sage Publications.

Volosinov, V. N. 1987. *Freudianism: A Critical Sketch*. Trans. I. R. Titunik. Bloomington: Indiana University Press.

Weibel, Kathryn. 1977. *Mirror Mirror: Images of Women Reflected in Popular Culture*. Garden City, N.Y.: Anchor Books.

Wernick, Andrew. 1991. *Promotional Culture*. London: Sage Publications.

Wildavsky, Aaron. 1982. "Conditions for a Pluralist Democracy or Cultural Pluralism Means More than One Political Culture in a Country." Unpublished paper.

Willemen, Paul. 1993. *Looks and Frictions: Essays in Cultural Studies and Film Theory.* Bloomington: Indiana University Press.

Williams, Raymond. 1958. *Culture and Society: 1780–1950.* New York: Columbia University Press.

———. 1976. *Keywords.* New York: Oxford University Press.

———. 1977. *Marxism and Literature.* New York: Oxford University Press.

Williams, Rosalind. 1990. *Notes on the Underground: An Essay on Technology, Society and the Imagination.* Cambridge, Mass.: MIT Press.

Williamson, Judith. 1978. *Decoding Advertisements: Ideology and Meaning in Advertising.* London: Marion Boyars.

Willis, Paul. 1990. *Common Culture: Symbolic Work at Play in the Everyday Cultures of the Young.* Boulder, Colo.: Westview.

Wilson, Clint C., and Felix Gutierrez. 1985. *Minorities and Media: Diversity and the End of Mass Communication.* Thousand Oaks, Calif.: Sage Publications.

Winick, Charles. 1994. *Desexualization in American Life: The New People.* New Brunswick, N.J.: Transaction.

Wollen, Peter. 1972. *Signs and Meaning in the Cinema.* Bloomington: Indiana University Press.

———. 1993. *Raiding the Icebox: Reflections on Twentieth-Century Culture.* Bloomington: Indiana University Press.

Wright, Will. 1975. *Sixguns and Society: A Structural Study of the Western.* Berkeley: University of California Press.

Zettl, Herbert. 1973. *Sight, Sound, Motion.* Belmont, Calif.: Wadsworth.

Zizek, Slavoi. 1991. *Looking Awry: An Introduction to Jacques Lacan through Popular Culture.* Cambridge, Mass.: MIT Press.

INDEX

ABOUT THE AUTHOR

Arthur Asa Berger is professor emeritus of Broadcast & Electronic Communication Arts at San Francisco State University, where he taught from 1965 until 2003. He was a Fulbright scholar at the University of Milan in 1963 and a visiting professor at the Annenberg School for Communication at the University of Southern California in 1984. He taught a short course on advertising and American culture at the Heinrich Heine University in Düsseldorf in 2002 as a Fulbright Senior Specialist and has lectured at more than a dozen universities in countries such as England, France, Finland, Brazil, Turkey, Thailand, and Vietnam. His books have been translated

into Italian, Swedish, German, Korean, Chinese, Turkish, Indonesian, and Arabic.

Berger has been writing about media and popular culture for almost fifty years. His MA thesis in 1956 was on the reception of the historian Arnold Toynbee in the American magazine press; his doctoral dissertation, in 1965, was on Al Capp's comic strip, *Li'l Abner*. His dissertation was published as *Li'l Abner: A Study in American Satire*. He has written fifty books and numerous articles and book reviews over the course of his career. He was in the Army from 1956 to 1958, and wrote on high school sports for the *Washington Post* during this period.

In recent years, Berger has written a number of comic academic novels that also function as textbooks: *Postmortem for a Postmodernist* (AltaMira Press), *The Mass Comm Murders: Five Media Theorists Self-Destruct* (Rowman & Littlefield), *Durkheim Is Dead: Sherlock Holmes Is Introduced to Social Theory* (AltaMira Press), and *The Hamlet Case* (Xlibris). His books are available on the Internet at sites such as Amazon.com and BN.com.

Berger is married to a philosophy professor, Phyllis Wolfson Berger, and has two children and two grandchildren. He lives in Mill Valley, California. He can be reached at aberger@sfsu.edu or arthurasaberger@yahoo.com.